AF610542

Jesus and the Brood of Vipers

Jesus and the Brood of Vipers
© copyright 2012 by Michael Jobling

ISBN 978-0-9565818-4-6

All rights reserved.

No part of this publication may be reproduced or transmitted in any form or by any means, electronic or mechanical, including photocopy, recording or any information storage or retrieval system, without permission in writing from the author.

Published by Treasure House Creative, Milton Keynes.

Cover photo © copyright A. Jaszlics, accessed from www.flickr.com under a creative commons license.

Unless otherwise indicated, quotations from the Bible are taken from the New International Version © copyright 2011, Biblica, formerly the International Bible Society, all rights reserved.

Contents

Chapter one

The Pure Ones

It is impossible to read the gospels without noticing the Pharisees. They crop up on almost every page, always in conflict with Jesus. With the exception of the money changers in the temple, they are the only people he condemns and, when he does condemn them, there are no half-measures. He verbally rips them to shreds.

When someone who is normally placid and easy-going raises his voice and uses forceful, aggressive language, you sit up and take notice. It means something is seriously wrong. The normally cheerful and calm nature of the person makes their sudden aggression more effective and striking. It shocks you because it is out of character. That's how it was with Jesus and the Pharisees. Jesus is normally so peaceful, loving and calm that, when we face his anger with the Pharisees, we find it hard to believe we are dealing with the same person. But there is a reason for the change. Several reasons, in fact, as we shall see.

Just as in the example of the normally placid person who suddenly blows their top, so it is with Jesus. The aggressive language he used to address the Pharisees seems initially out of character. Think about it – normally, Jesus showed kindness and compassion to people others wouldn't give the time of day to. Adulteresses and immoral people were brought to him during the course of his ministry. He treated each of them kindly. It was the same with the tax collectors. In Jesus' day you couldn't get lower than a tax collector. Tax collectors were the most loathed people in the community. The Roman government contracted tax collection out to the private sector. As long as the government received the income it wanted, it was up to the tax collectors how they obtained it from the population. They were allowed to add on as much as they wanted to cover their own costs and give them a profit. People resented them and regarded them as traitors – cruel, corrupt, freelance opportunists out for a fast buck. But Jesus was nice to them. He even invited himself to a meal with one. He was polite and welcoming to Roman soldiers, he allowed terrorist freedom fighters into the circle of his disciples, and told the dying thief he would go to paradise. But Pharisees were a different matter. He called them "whitewashed tombs", "a brood of vipers" and "children of the devil". He hardy had a good word for them. They, on the other hand, plotted to kill him.

This is all the more amazing when you realise that the Pharisees were the upholders of the Law of Moses, the guardians of public morality. It was like Cliff Richard having a major feud with the leaders of the Evangelical Alliance and enraging them so much that they plotted to have him assassinated. Or the leaders of the Southern Baptist denomination wanting to put Tony Campolo on death row. Why did the Pharisees hate Jesus? Why was he so implacably opposed to them? And who were they, anyway?

The Pharisees were one of two major parties within Judaism at the time of Jesus. They had their origin in the period of history between the Old and New Testaments. But to get to the root of the Pharisee movement you have to go back into the Old Testament, to the book of Psalms, where there are frequent references to people called in Hebrew the *Hasidim*. The name means "The loyal ones". In English Bibles it is translated as "saints", "holy ones" the "consecrated ones" or "the righteous". Psalm 50 v 4 and 5 is a good example:

> "He summons the heavens above
> and the earth, that he may judge his people:
> 'Gather to me this *consecrated people*
> Who made a covenant with me by sacrifice.' "

The *hasidim* are people who are loyal to God and his laws. These references to the righteous ones became an inspiration to the supporters of a new movement which grew up during the second century BC. It consisted of Jewish people who began to apply that title from the Psalms to themselves. They aspired to be the "loyal ones" the scriptures referred to. They lived at a time when Greek culture and philosophy were having a considerable influence on the Jewish community. A while before, Alexander the Great had conquered the Jews and Judea had become part of the Greek empire. The influence of Greek language and culture became very strong, and lingered for centuries after, right into New Testament times. As Greek culture eroded Jewish identity more and more, a popular resistance movement grew, drawing together people who opposed the incursion of pagan ways and wanted to remain faithful to God's laws. These people were the forerunners of the Pharisees we meet in the New Testament. They had a majority following, and tried to wrest control of Jerusalem from the powerful, Greek-sympathising minority who held the power. In an attempt to re-establish control over Jerusalem, the Greek-sympathising rulers put down the *hasidim* with help from the Syrian King, Antiochus Epiphanes.

Antiochus was successful in this venture and deposed a High Priest called Onias III, who seems to have been the leader of the *hasidim*. This was a turning point. To begin with, the *hasidim* had been non-violent, but Antiochus was so repressive and insensitive to these traditional Jews that they resorted to force. A series of conflicts resulted known as the Maccabean wars, in which the *hasidim* played a major part. Initially they and their supporters were successful, and managed to win back from the Syrians almost all the territory that had belonged to David's kingdom. They ruthlessly subjected the population to their control and forced every male to be circumcised.

As far as we can see, the *hasidim* movement continued and lasted on into New Testament times to become the Pharisee party of Jesus' day. Somewhere along the line they took on the new name, "Pharisees", the meaning of which is a little uncertain. One theory is that it means "the pure ones". Another likely explanation is that the name came from an Aramaic word that had to do with division or separation (in Jesus' time ordinary people in that part of the world spoke Aramaic). The Pharisees were thus "the separated ones". They stood in opposition to another group, the Sadducees, who had a more easygoing and liberal outlook. The Pharisees prided themselves on keeping separate from the world and its sinful ways, preserving their distinctive Jewish identity and being loyal to God and to his laws. They believed that the Babylonian exile had been caused by the failure of the Jewish nation to keep the *Torah*, the Law of God. They were concerned to make sure that nothing like that ever happened again. To this end they did two things. One was to attempt to define the law as accurately and meticulously as possible so that there would never be any doubt about whether a particular action broke the law or not. The other thing they did to safeguard against lawbreaking was to create a new set of man-made laws which were even more stringent than the Law of Moses. They thought of the Law of God as if it were a cliff which it was possible to fall over. Just as you might erect a fence a safe distance back from the edge of the cliff to ensure that no-one fell over it, they tried to put a "hedge" round the law by making laws which were actually more strict than God required. They hoped that by keeping the stricter, man-made version, they would be certain not to fall foul of the less severe version of the law that God had actually given. They summarised the law in 613 commandments. 248 of these were positive and 365 were negative. They also believed that the law consisted not only of fixed commandments, but of also principles which could be extended to give guidance for living in every conceivable situation. They believed that, by studying the law carefully and discussing it, they could infer God's will for new situations which the laws in the Old Testament did not specifically cover. A majority opinion on the interpretation and application of the law was binding on the whole Pharisee community. This was not a discussion group which was open to consider new ideas – if you didn't toe the line, you were out.

So what was wrong with that? Their motive was to honour God and keep His law. Surely it was a good thing to go to such lengths to be righteous? The Pharisees were good Jews, godly Jews, enthusiastic, devoted and disciplined. They were the very people you would expect the Son of God to approve of – the very people you would expect to approve of him. Yet Jesus and the Pharisees were constantly at loggerheads. In fact, as we shall see, it was the Pharisees who were largely responsible for his death.

They were a very influential group of people. There were about 6,000 * of them in Palestine during the reign of King Herod. They were particularly well-represented among the priests and scribes, but had many lay people in their number as well. They enjoyed support and respect from many in the community who wouldn't actually join them in a formal sense. They tended to trade and intermarry among themselves, in order to keep pure, and so had a strong network of mutual support. In those days in Judaea, if you got on the wrong side of the Pharisees you were finished. And Jesus managed to earn their disapproval, to the extent that they began to plot to kill him. Given the strength of their representation among the priests, it was almost certainly pressure and string-pulling by the Pharisees that led the Chief Priest and the rulers of the Jewish Council to arrest Jesus, try him and take him to Pilate for permission to have him executed.

So Jesus, the Son of God, somehow managed to so upset the most God-fearing and righteous people in the land that they were out for his blood. That must surely surprise us. What was it about Jesus that angered the Pharisees so much and what was it about them that angered him? What were the issues of disagreement between them?

It is a question worth pursuing. A noted biblical scholar of the nineteenth century, William Smith, wrote in his *Dictionary of the Bible* in 1863,

> "to understand the Pharisees is by contrast an aid toward understanding the spirit of uncorrupted Christianity."

In other words, find out about the Pharisees, discover where Jesus disagreed with them, and in the process you'll get to the heart of Jesus himself. That's the aim of this book. In the following pages we are going to look in detail at the areas of disagreement between the Pharisees and Jesus, to analyse the points where they differed. We are going to trace the course of the conflict between them, and in the process learn some lessons which will help us follow Jesus Christ more closely today. The implications for Christians today are far reaching, because what we shall find is that the Pharisees are not just a bunch of fanatics who lived a long time ago. The spirit of the Pharisee movement still lives on and there are Pharisees around today. You may well find yourself sitting beside one next time you go to church. In fact it comes closer than that, because each of us, if we are honest, has a bit of the Pharisee in us.

* Information about the Pharisees and the Jewish population in the first century AD is largely sourced from *Jerusalem in the Time of Jesus* by Joachim Jeremias published by SCM in1969.

Chapter two

The Heart of the Matter

If you want to understand the conflict between Jesus and the Pharisees, a good place to start is the Sermon on the Mount, universally recognised as the summary of Jesus' teaching. It contains several references to the Pharisees, some where Jesus directly contrasts his teaching with theirs. These provide us with insight into the main areas of conflict between him and them.

According to Matthew (the most Jewish of Jesus' four biographers), Jesus delivered the Sermon on the Mount, as it is now known, sitting with his disciples on a hillside overlooking the Sea of Galilee, soon after the beginning of his three years of ministry. It has been called Jesus' manifesto. It brings us closer to the heart of Jesus than any other passage in the Bible. You'll find it recorded in Matthew chapters 5–7.

Before we examine it in the light of the conflict between Jesus and the Pharisees, let me give an overview to remind ourselves what the Sermon on the Mount was about. Feel free to skip this part if you don't need to be reminded!

The sermon divides into four sections, listed on the next few pages.

Section 1 – The Beatitudes (Matthew 5 v. 3–12)

The Beatitudes are nine statements, each of which begins with the words "Blessed are..." (or in some modern translations, "Happy are...".) It is probably true to say that most people who read the Beatitudes today misunderstand them. Almost always, when I quiz people about their understanding of the Beatitudes I find they have imposed on this part of Jesus' teaching a false expectation that sermons are about telling people what they should do. As a result, they understand these statements as law, as if Jesus were saying, "You must be like this if you want to be blessed." This is actually the opposite of what Jesus intended. The Beatitudes are about what God intends to do, not what he wants *us* to do. They are a proclamation of the merciful acts of God which are going to take place as God establishes his kingdom. Jesus is saying ,"Now that the kingdom of God is coming, people are going to be blessed in the following ways, according to their needs." For example, "Blessed are the poor in spirit, for theirs is the kingdom of Heaven" doesn't mean, "You must be poor in spirit, because you won't get to Heaven if you aren't." That's not what Jesus is saying here at all. What it does mean is,

> "When the Kingdom of Heaven comes, those who are poor in spirit are going to receive all its benefits."

Similarly, when the kingdom comes, those who are mourning will be comforted, those who are humble will be put in charge of things, those who have been longing for righteousness will have their desire met, and so on. The whole thing is a declaration of God's intention to turn the world upside down and redress the wrongs that have taken place. It isn't law, it is gospel – good news.

The beatitudes end with Jesus speaking specifically to his disciples:

> "Blessed are you, when people insult you, persecute you and falsely say all kinds of evil things against you because of me. Rejoice and be glad because great is your reward in Heaven..." (Matthew 5 v 11–12)

Section 2 – A statement to the disciples about their importance (Matthew 5: v 13–14)

After the Beatitudes, Jesus goes on to use three images that illustrate the task facing his disciples. They are to be like salt, like light and like a city on a hilltop.

Section 4 – Instructions about how the disciples are to live (Matthew 6–7)

I'm saving Section 3 until last, because this is where the Pharisees come in. The Sermon on the Mount ends with teaching about how Jesus' disciples are to live (Matthew 6–7). This includes instructions about giving to the poor, prayer and fasting, about not laying up treasure on earth, and not judging and condemning others. Jesus summarises the attitude he wants his disciples to have in the words,

> "Do to others what you would have them do to you, for this sums up the Law and the Prophets." (Matthew 7 v 12)

He rounds the whole thing off with the parable of the wise and foolish builders and the punchline, "Therefore everyone who hears these words of mine and puts them into practice is like a wise man who built his house on a rock."

Section 3 Jesus' approach contrasted with that of the Pharisees (Matthew 5 v 17–47)

In between illustrating the disciples' role and giving them instructions about how to live, Jesus takes time to contrast his approach with that of the Pharisees and explains his attitude to the Law. Matthew 5, verse 20 gives us the key to understanding this section:

> "For I tell you that, unless your righteousness surpasses that of the Pharisees and the teachers of the law, you will certainly not enter the kingdom of Heaven."

As we can see from this verse, the problem Jesus had with the Pharisees was not that they were too strict, but that they were not strict enough!

In no way does Jesus want to minimise or remove the standard of righteousness and holiness that the Pharisees set. On the contrary, he wants to see people keeping an even higher standard:

> "Do not think that I have come to abolish the Law or the Prophets. I have not come to abolish them but to fulfil them. I tell you the truth, until heaven and earth disappear, not the smallest letter, not the least stroke of a pen, will by any means disappear from the Law until everything is accomplished."
>
> (Matthew 5 v 17–18)

Here's an interesting question: The Pharisees were the most meticulous and assiduous keepers of the Law ever. No-one before them or since has ever kept the Old Testament Law better. They observed the smallest detail and endured tremendous personal inconvenience to honour God by keeping his laws. They would have heated discussions about the precise definition of "work" so they could make sure that they wouldn't break the commandment by working on the Sabbath. How then is it possible for the disciples' righteousness to exceed theirs?

The disciples must have groaned inwardly and felt like giving up when Jesus talked about exceeding the righteousness of the Pharisees! Imagine the equivalent demand in other contexts: "You must run further and faster than Paula Radcliffe or Usain Bolt. You must sing better than Pavarotti, beat Nadal at tennis." The reaction you have to those demands must be how the disciples felt about the idea of being more righteous than the Pharisees. "How can you be better than the best?"

However, what follows in the Sermon on the Mount gives a clue to what Jesus meant. It is revolutionary, not only against the background of Jesus' day, but in today's context as well. In fact, although the Sermon on the Mount has been around for about 2,000 years, I think it would be true to say that the majority of Jesus' followers have still not really grasped it.

Jesus follows his stunning statement about exceeding the righteousness of the Pharisees with a series of statements each of which follows the same formula:

> "You have heard that it was said to the people long ago… but I tell you…."

He reaffirms the main points of the Old Testament laws about murder, adultery, divorce, breaking oaths, excessive vengeance, and love for one's neighbour, but at the same time he gives each of them a twist of his own.

Some commentators suggest that by going up a hill to deliver this manifesto Jesus deliberately created a parallel with Moses giving the law on Mt. Sinai, so setting his teaching up in direct opposition to the law of Moses. In each case the difference between the traditional understanding of the law and the "new law" that Jesus gives boils down to three key issues:

1. Which is more important, the act or the motive?
2. Which is more important, the rule or the result? and
3. What should be the main intention of the law, to avoid evil or promote goodness?

1. Which is more important, the act or the motive?

As the Pharisees understood it the Law was concerned with actions. Everyone else understood it that way at that time and most people understand it that way today – God had decreed that certain actions were good, and others were wrong. He had set penalties to pay for breaking his laws and rewards to for those who kept them. The Pharisees therefore understood that, if you did what was wrong, or even if you failed to do what was right, you could expect God to judge and condemn you. On the other hand, if you did what was right, you could expect to be rewarded. *Why* you did what was right or wrong was a secondary consideration. The important thing was *what* you did.

But Jesus moved the goalposts. In Jesus' teaching it is the motive which is important, rather than the action. Right motives will normally lead to right actions, but right actions do not justify wrong motives. Jesus even opened up the possibility that right motives might justify apparently wrong actions, especially when those actions achieve positive and beneficial results. The Pharisees found this hard to swallow.

Although they found this approach hard to accept, it was actually nothing new. The seed of it is already there in the Old Testament, in the principle upon which God chose Israel's first King:

> "Do not consider his appearance or his height, for I have rejected him. The Lord does not look at the things people look at. People look at the outward appearance, but the Lord looks at the heart." (1 Samuel 16 v 7)

God judges the heart, not just the outward appearance. That means he does not just judge what we do, but why we do it. Consequently Jesus' new law condemns not actions, but attitudes. Take the question of murder, for example:

> "You have heard that it was said to the people long ago, 'Do not murder', and 'anyone who murders will be subject to judgement.' But I tell you that anyone who is angry with his brother will be subject to judgement." (Matthew 5 v 21–22)

Even under the strict morality of the Pharisees it was possible to hate someone with impunity. Indeed, they actively encouraged hatred of sinners – after all, what attitude could be more appropriate towards someone who disobeyed God's laws? And even if the anger was purely selfish, arising out of some felt insult or an offence against your own pride or dignity, provided you didn't cause injury to the person you were angry with, there was nothing wrong in anger. But Jesus says simply, "No anger. No hatred. If you give in to anger you get judged for it."

Psychologists observe a dynamic in the interaction between people which they call projection. This relates to the gap between people's intentions, and their actions. Let's say that you start off with an intention: something you want to achieve, or do or say. Nearly always the result of your actions will fall short of what you intend, sometimes without you being aware of it. Someone else then observes what you do, or hears what you say, and thinks, "What would I have intended, in order to produce that behaviour?" They then assume that what happened is what you wanted to happen, or that what you say is what you meant to say. They project that understanding of your motive on to you, like a film projector imposing an image on a screen. They impute those intentions to you, though it is a misconception of what your real motives were.

Every day millions of disagreements occur between people caught in the same trap of misunderstanding. One person feels resentment and hurt because of non-existent intentions that they imagine the other person to have had and then the other person feels misjudged. But God never misunderstands. He knows the intentions of our heart, and it is those that he judges. Jesus judged with God's perfect judgement. That was how he could on the one hand be so gentle and lenient with the woman caught in the act of adultery and yet, in the Sermon on the Mount, command us to be resolute and uncompromising in rooting sexual immorality out of our lives:

> "If your right eye causes you to sin, gouge it out and throw it away ..." (Matthew 5 v 29)

It is the intention that God judges, rather than the act. So Jesus is entirely consistent in both encouraging a thorough holiness which comes from the heart while at the same time showing lenience to people who, while they have sinned in act, have done so with pardonable, or at least excusable intentions. The law condemned the physical act of adultery. But Jesus says:

> "I tell you that anyone who looks at a woman lustfully has already committed adultery with her in his heart."
> (Matthew 5 v 28)

I assume that Jesus was talking here to male disciples. In mixed company, would he have expressed the same principle in a more balanced way? Women are not incapable of lust. There may be generalised differences in the kinds of lust to which each sex is particularly prone, but both are capable of desiring either love, comfort and companionship or physical pleasure. Jesus makes it clear that the physical act of sex, whether viewed from a male or female perspective, is of only secondary concern to God because sexual activity is merely the outward expression of what is already present in a person's heart and intention. It is what goes on inside a person's mind that God judges rather than what they do with their bodies. Of course those who physically commit adultery are guilty before God but so is anyone who has considered it and, even for a moment, thought with interest and desire about the possibility of committing adultery. By Jesus' law they are just as guilty as those who actually do it. Indeed, adulterers who admit and regret their adultery may be more in God's favour than others who have never committed the act and refuse to admit to the secret desire concealed in their heart.

I think that, if they are honest, most Christians have a view of sexual morality which makes a distinction between the act and the desire. Looking lustfully is bad, we think, and we must try not to do it, but if we manage to stop short of acting on lustful impulses and desires we are doing well – committing adultery is worse than thinking about it. But Jesus takes another view. He makes it plain that it is not the act of adultery which God judges, but the attitudes of heart which lead to it – not only lust, but selfishness, lack of concern for other people's pain, and the degrading of others into objects to be manipulated for emotional comfort or physical pleasure. That doesn't mean that adulterers can excuse themselves by saying, "I'm only being honest in giving expression to what is in my mind anyway." If it is in your mind, God doesn't want it to stay there – he wants to help you to remove it so that the compulsion to do it is no longer there.

On these two issues alone Christians today are often in conflict with the law of Jesus. How many churches have been rent apart by animosities between opposing parties, cherishing in their hearts attitudes which, according to Jesus, God views as seriously as the act of murder? How often are Christians who have committed sexual sin, even when they are repentant, rejected by others who, if they are honest, have secretly cherished romantic or sexual fantasies which make them as guilty in God's eyes as the person who has physically committed adultery?

The same principle runs through all the statements. For instance it is not the act of divorce which God condemns, but the inward attitude of rejection behind it. Oaths are necessary only because people sometimes do not mean what they say. Rather than saying "Keep your oaths," Jesus says, "Say what you mean and keep your word."

Towards the end of the Sermon on the Mount Jesus used the image of a tree bearing fruit to express his view of righteousness. The deeds people do are the fruit of the kind of person they are:

> "A good tree cannot bear bad fruit, and a bad tree cannot bear good fruit." (Matthew 7 v 18)

The key to righteousness is thus in changing the tree, in other words a person's heart, rather than trying to make apple trees produce pears!

The most clear contrast between Jesus' approach and the Pharisees probably comes in an incident which is recorded in both Matthew 15 and Mark 7. The initiative in this incident was with the Pharisees. Mark explains the background to the confrontation for the sake of Gentiles who weren't in the know about Jewish customs:

> "The Pharisees, and all the Jews, do not eat unless they give their hands a ceremonial washing, holding to the tradition of the elders. When they come from the market-place they do not eat unless they wash. And they observe many other traditions, such as the washing of cups, pitchers and kettles." (Mark 7 v 3–4)

The point of all this washing was to make sure that they did not inadvertently break any of the Old Testament laws about diet or hygiene by eating while they had traces of forbidden substances on their hands or in their cups and plates. The Pharisees noticed that Jesus' disciples were less than meticulous in this area, so they sent a representative with an accusing question for Jesus:

> "Why do your disciples break the tradition of the elders? They don't wash their hands before they eat!" (Matthew 15 v 2)

As part of his response to this, Jesus set forward a principle:

> "Listen and understand. What goes into a someone's mouth does not defile them but what comes out of their mouth, that is what defiles them."
> (Matthew 15 v 10)

Afterwards, Jesus' disciples said to him, "Do you know that the Pharisees were offended when they heard this?" The Pharisees' reaction is interesting, assuming the disciples read it right. What exactly does "offended" mean? Did they think that Jesus was calling them unclean? Were they just shocked by the casual way Jesus dismissed the question, and with it the whole issue of ceremonial washing? Jesus obviously unsettled them – and unsettled the disciples, too. The effect of what Jesus said would be similar to the effect of telling a modern-day group of Christians not to bother about going to church on Sunday. The disciples weren't quite sure if they had heard what they thought they heard. And if it meant what they thought it meant, it wasn't what they were expecting Jesus to say. So Peter said to Jesus, in effect: "Can you just run that by me one more time, Lord, I'm not sure if I quite got it?"

Jesus then repeated the principle, this time spelling it out more clearly:

> "Don't you see that whatever enters the mouth goes into the stomach and then out of the body? But the things that come out of a person's mouth come from the heart, and these defile them. For out of the heart come evil thoughts, murder, adultery, sexual immorality, theft, false testimony, slander. These are what defile a person." (Matthew 15 v 17–20)

The Pharisees thought of themselves as clean. They were the pure, separated ones who didn't break God's law. They needed to make every effort to avoid being contaminated by the world around them. They saw defilement as coming from outside – not just the physical defilement which might enter through unwashed cups and plates, but also the moral pollution which came from contact with sinners around them.

Jesus, on the other hand, saw uncleanness as something which resided in the human heart, defiling people from within. In Jesus' view, the world cannot make people more sinful or corrupt than they already are in their own hearts. Sinfulness in others may unlock the sinfulness in our own hearts, but it doesn't put it there.

The Pharisees failed to grasp this, but it was the starting point of all Jesus' dealings with sin and sinners. Earlier, I said that the differences between Jesus and the Pharisees boiled down to three basic issues. We have examined the first, the issue of motive or action, the heart or the outward appearance. We now move on to the second.

2. Which is more important, the rule or the result?

Here Jesus doesn't just move the goalposts. What he says is almost like setting up new goalposts at the other end of the field – changing the game, even. Jesus made it plain that God judges us, not only by the motivation of our hearts, but also by the results of our actions – the effect they have on others.

The Pharisees' focus was on observing the law as written. It didn't matter to them whether their observance of the law helped or harmed anyone else. The important thing was that you did what the law said. Jesus points us beyond this to consider the effect of our actions on others. It isn't enough simply to avoid anger and murder. Goodness involves going beyond that to seek reconciliation:

> "Therefore if you are offering your gift at the altar, and there remember that your brother or sister has something against you, leave your gift there in front of the altar. First go and be reconciled to them; then come and offer your gift."
>
> (Matthew 5 v 23)

Again, when it comes to divorce, Jesus takes the result of people's actions into consideration. One of the reasons why divorce is sinful is because of the spiritual, emotional and economic effects on the person who is rejected by divorce. In New Testament times the wife who was sent away with a bill of divorce would have been forced to marry again and be branded as an adulteress, or even to become a prostitute in order to survive. Economic necessity would have forced her to become bound to another man or to seek her livelihood from other men. It was unacceptable, in Jesus' eyes, to force this situation onto a woman, even though the law made provision for divorce. Jesus judged, not whether someone had stayed within the law, but whether their action had the aim of giving glory to God and helping other people. No matter how legal the action, if it sprang from wrong motives and the result of it was that harm came to others, then Jesus condemned it. On the other hand, even though an action broke the law, if the perpetrator of it intended good and it brought good to others, Jesus pardoned it.

3. Which is the purpose of the law, to avoid evil or to promote good?

The third difference between Jesus and the Pharisees relates to the focus of the Law. Jesus' focus was positive, the Pharisees' focus was negative. For them, the Law was about avoiding sin. Again, Jesus moved the goalposts. The Law, in Jesus' eyes, is only fulfilled by the pursuit of active goodness. The law restricted the payment that you could exact from someone who had offended you. It had to be in proportion to the offence – "eye for eye and tooth for tooth" was the way Moses had put it, which is another way of saying, "Let the punishment fit the crime." In contrast, Jesus' law requires us to seek active goodness – to offer the other cheek when you are struck; when a soldier forces you to carry his pack for a mile to volunteer to carry it another mile; to give to those who ask you; to love your enemy as well as your neighbour; to pray for those who persecute you. The Pharisees were satisfied with just obeying God. Jesus set us the higher aim of becoming like him:

> "Be perfect, therefore, as your heavenly Father is perfect."
> (Matthew 5 v 48)

An impossible dream?

"But that's impossible!" – that must surely have been the reaction of the disciples to Jesus' words as they sat on the hillside listening to him.

There's no hint that any of them interrupted him to point out how unattainable was the standard of righteousness that he was setting. Perhaps they were just too stunned to make any response! How can anyone hope to avoid sinning, if God judges people according to Jesus' law as set out in the Sermon on the Mount? We stand a chance, if only a remote one, of adhering to an external code of ethics, but to have total control of our thoughts and emotions, never to even think a wrong thought, even for a second, and never to feel a wrong desire – well, that's just impossible.

But, of course, that's the whole point. Thirty years or so later, the Apostle Paul, writing to the Roman Christians, was to quote some words from the Psalms to express the same understanding:

> "There is no-one righteous, not even one;
> There is no-one who understands,
> No-one who seeks God.
> All have turned away, they have together become worthless;
> There is no-one who does good, not even one."
>
> (Romans 3 v 10–12)

The Pharisees' understanding of the Law left just a tiny hope that it might be possible through human effort to keep the law and thus to be counted as righteous. In contrast, Jesus' law left no place for self-effort. It exposed the sinfulness of the human heart which will still be there even in a person who keeps the law in meticulous detail. Jesus' declaration of his new law in the Sermon on the Mount prepared the way for the message of grace and mercy that he came to bring, the message that God is ushering in a new regime and that one of the benefits of this new administration is pardon and mercy for human beings whose hearts have been corrupted by sin and who could never hope to be good enough to escape God's judgement.

At the same time, Jesus' law prepared the way for a new kind of goodness, a goodness which is positive rather than negative – concerned with giving blessings rather than exacting penalties. This is a goodness that springs from a heart that the Holy Spirit has purified and empowered and which, full of gratitude for mercy received, wants to show mercy to others.

By insisting on their kind of righteousness the Pharisees were standing in the way of people receiving the blessings of the coming Kingdom of God. Consequently, Jesus had to oppose them – and that was where the conflict began.

Chapter three

Why Be Good?

Once you go beyond the mere act of obedience to God's law and apply that law to the heart, the question of motives becomes vitally important. Pharisees could have unworthy motives for doing things that, on the surface, seemed praiseworthy. Jesus was ruthless in searching out these hidden motives and bringing them to light. The Pharisees were not much bothered why you did something, so long as you did the right thing. But, for Jesus, having the right motive was vitally important. Again, the difference is very evident in the Sermon on the Mount. In Matthew 6, Jesus contrasts the way the disciples are to behave with the behaviour of some people he refers to as "the hypocrites". Jesus doesn't use the name "Pharisee" at this point, but the practices he describes would be recognised by his hearers as common among the Pharisee party: giving alms, praying long prayers, and fasting. The "hypocrites" Jesus referred to put on an outward show of goodness, in order to impress other people. He says:

> "Be careful not to practice your acts of righteousnessin front of others, *to be seen by them*."
>
> "So when you give to the needy, do not announce it with trumpets, as the hypocrites do in the synagogues and on the streets *to be honoured by others*."

> "And when you pray, do not be like the hypocrites, for they love to pray standing in the synagogues and on the street corners *to be seen by others*." (Matthew 6 v 1, 2, 5, my emphasis).

The "hypocrites" Jesus describes have a hidden motive in their apparent goodness. They are being good in order to gain praise and acceptance from other people. Jesus said some very similar things in Matthew, chapter 23.

> "Everything they do is done for men to see: they make heir phylacteries wide and the tassels on their garments long; they love the place of honour at banquets and the most important seats in the synagogues; they love to be greeted with respect in the market places and to be called 'Rabbi' by others.
> (Matthew 23 v 5–7)

It's easy for us to look with disdain at the hypocritical Pharisees in Jesus' caricature, but there is more of the hypocritical Pharisee in most of us than we would care to admit. It may be that our motive for goodness is more to avoid the rejection and disapproval of others than to gain "brownie points" but the motive is still a selfish one, with basically the same orientation: if you are "good", people will like you. They don't like you if you are bad, so you try to be good. We learn the lesson early in childhood. We discover that certain actions bring the reward of loving attention from our parents or others around us, while other actions bring anger and even violence down on our heads. We soon learn to co-operate and to do business, trading our compliance for whatever rewards are on offer. If your parents have put their love on the line and hinted that they will stop loving you unless you behave/keep quiet/do well at school, your eagerness to please, and your fear of failing, will be that much stronger.

Psychotherapists sometimes use the phrase "performance orientation" to describe this outlook, and "conditional love" for the parental approach which brings it about. The Pharisees were largely motivated by performance orientation. They supposed that God's love was conditional. As a result they geared their whole life to the task of convincing God that they were good enough.

In Jesus' parable of the Pharisee and the tax collector (Luke 18 v 9–14) Jesus illustrates this. The Pharisee composes his prayer in such a way as to remind God how good he had been (in case God hadn't noticed, or had forgotten!). He hadn't stolen, cheated or committed adultery, he fasted twice a week and paid his tithes in full. He obviously expected that all this would gain him God's approval and make it more likely that God would answer his prayers. The Pharisees assumed that by keeping the law in meticulous detail they would retain God's approval and favour, and that by breaking the law, they would incur his anger and rejection.

Where did this understanding come from? It wasn't something God had revealed to them. It was an assumption they made about God. They assumed that God would deal with them in this way, because that was what they experienced from their fellow men, and the way they treated each other. If you didn't keep the law properly, you couldn't be a Pharisee. So to God's disapproval would be added the disapproval of your fellow Pharisees. Since the Pharisees were good at showing disapproval, this was a powerful motivation for "keeping your nose clean". Consequently, on the whole, the Pharisees ended up being an extremely law-abiding group of people. But this was only a superficial veneer. Under the surface, they were riddled with fear, scared of making a false move that would bring a pointing finger from other Pharisees. Although they kept the law outwardly with some success because they were desperately afraid of breaking it, in their minds they were not nearly so careful.

It is impossible to live in fear without experiencing stress and feeling bad about yourself. If you constantly feel bad about yourself, you become hungry for approval and affirmation. Consequently Pharisees became eager to wring the last ounce of recognition and approval from others around them, seeking the seats of honour at banquets, the best places at the synagogue, cherishing titles which gave them respect and recognition. Theirs was a neurotic religion. They lived in a trap, caught between intense fear of rejection on the one hand, and craving for approval on the other.

In an aside in Luke 16 v 14, Luke says that the Pharisees "loved money". They saw prosperity as a sign of favour, a reward for being good. That meant that it would also bring approval from others, especially fellow Pharisees. This brought the temptation to use devious means to obtain the wealth which would give the outward appearance of being favoured by God, and hence draw the favour of men.

The Pharisees saw good health, similarly, as a sign of God's favour. This may be behind their less than approving reaction to Jesus' healing miracles, especially those that took place on the Sabbath. They assumed that sick people had incurred God's displeasure by some neglect in keeping the law. God would heal them in his time if they repented and were good enough. The Pharisees would have thought it presumptuous in the extreme for Jesus to come and heal such people on the spot, especially if he did it without strong admonitions about being good and avoiding God's displeasure in the future.

You can see this interaction quite clearly in the healing of the paralysed man in Mark 2 v 1–12. Rather than healing the man in the first instance, Jesus said "Son, your sins are forgiven." The Pharisees were horrified:

> "Now some teachers of the law were sitting there, thinking to themselves. 'Why does this fellow talk like that? He's blaspheming! Who can forgive sins but God alone?"
>
> (Mark 2 v 6 & 7)

Because of the way the Pharisees viewed illness, Jesus was able to use the healing of the man as evidence to show that He really did (and does!) have authority from God to forgive sins:

> " '... But I want you to know that the Son of Man has authority on earth to forgive sins.' So he said to the man, 'I tell you, get up, take your mat and go home.' " (Mark 2 v 11)

For Jesus, goodness is not goodness unless it is unselfish. You may keep the law in every detail, but if your motive is self-advantage, your law-keeping is disqualified. All the kind or law-abiding things you do are worth nothing if your only aim in doing them is to get people to love you.

There are only two right motives for being good. Jesus laid them out clearly on one occasion in response to a question by one of the Pharisees.

> " Hearing that Jesus had silenced the Saducees, the Pharisees got together. One of them, an expert in the law, tested him with this question: 'Teacher, which is the greatest commandment in the Law?' Jesus replied: '"Love the Lord your God with all your heart and with all your soul and with all your mind". This is the first and greatest commandment. And the second is like it: "Love your neighbour as yourself." All the Law and the Prophets hang on these two commandments.'" (Matthew 22 v 35)

Notice the assumption behind the Pharisee's question. He assumes there can be a conflict between the demands of one law and the demands of another. In that situation it is important to know which law takes precedence. Otherwise, how are you to know how best to gain God's favour?

Jesus' answer, typically, takes a step back from the act of law keeping or law breaking, and looks at the motivation involved. The motive of the heart is the key to discerning the comparative priority of different laws. The two laws Jesus selects as the most important both deal with the heart. The first and most important motive for being good is a response of love to God, and the second is an attitude of love towards your neighbour. In Jesus' view, we should keep the Law, not to make God love us, but because we already love Him. Not keeping the law will normally be an evidence of lack of love for God. However, it is not always true that the person who does keep the law loves God. There are other reasons for keeping it. For the Pharisees, goodness was a currency. Their understanding was that you do good so as to get good back and you return favours when people do favours for you. But if you follow Jesus' approach, you begin with the respect, honour, love and gratitude that we owe to God, because he is God and we are bound to obey him. The Laws are his laws, so we keep them to honour him. Other people are his creatures, and he loves them, so we treat them with honour and respect too. We don't act towards them with kindness to persuade them to like us in return, but because they are

God's creatures and we know that he loves them. For Jesus, goodness is an act of worship. It is a response to who and what God is.

This thought of passing on God's love and goodness runs as a thread through all of Jesus' teaching. When he sent out the disciples on their preaching missions he said

> " Freely you have received, freely give." (Matthew 10 v 8)

They don't need to receive anything in return for their good deeds because the good deeds are being supplied by God. There is no possibility of them experiencing loss through acts of mercy or kindness, because they are simply passing on the kindness that God has shown to them.

"Your Father in Heaven," says Jesus in the Sermon on the Mount, "causes his sun to rise on the evil and the good, and sends rain on the righteous and the unrighteous." (Matthew 5 v 45). God gives generously and unconditionally to bad and good alike. We are to pass on God's goodness by acting with kindness and mercy, not only to those who are nice to us, but also to our enemies and people who persecute us.

Forgiveness too is something which we pass on because we receive it from God:

> " For if you forgive other people when they sin against you, your Heavenly Father will also forgive you." (Matthew 6 v 14)

This is not to say that God does not reward goodness. On the contrary, there are several passages in the gospels where Jesus promises rewards from God. God will reward you for the gifts you give in secret, and he will answer your secret prayers – Jesus promises this in Matthew 6 v 3–6. But God rewards not the act of giving or praying, but the motive and attitude of heart in which it is done. All the good deeds of the proud Pharisee in Luke 18 v 9 were insufficient to get him any reward from God, but God rewarded the humble heart of the tax collector:

> " I tell you that this man, rather than the other, went home justified before God." (Luke 18 v 14)

Chapter four

Praise and Blame

Every parent and teacher, to be successful, needs to learn the power of praise. Students and children always respond better to praise than they do to nagging and criticism. There is a place for loving confrontation and correction but reinforcing good behaviour with praise is usually much more effective.

For most people, praise does not come naturally. Many of us find it easier to live with criticism and complaint than with praise. If you listen to most of the conversations which go on around you, you'll find the language of complaint is widely used while the language of praise is like a strange, minority dialect. People are always complaining – about the weather, the government, the boss, their children, their parents and so on. Children usually have to be taught to be appreciative and grateful. Complaining comes naturally.

This leads us to a further important difference between Jesus and the Pharisees. Jesus was noticeably free with praise and avoided condemning people (with the one exception of the Pharisees, whom he condemned for being condemning). Jesus' approach was almost always to affirm and praise the good in people, while the Pharisees' outlook was at root a critical one. The evidence in the gospels suggests that the

Pharisees were always looking for opportunities to pick holes in other people's performance, to point out their failures, and castigate their wrongdoing.

A quick review of some encounters between Jesus and Pharisees in the gospels serves to illustrate the Pharisees' negative attitude. Of course Jesus himself was the butt of much of their criticism. They criticised him for eating with tax-collectors and sinners, for not encouraging his disciples to fast (Mark 3), for eating without washing his hands (Mark 7), for allowing his disciples to pick ears of corn on the Sabbath (Luke 6), for not paying the temple tax (Matthew 16) and for healing on the Sabbath. (John 9). And, rather than rejoicing at the authority Jesus showed over demons, the Pharisees accused him of being able to cast out demons because he was in league with them (Matthew 12).

However, Jesus wasn't the only butt of their criticism. It was a Pharisee who criticised the woman who anointed Jesus' feet with ointment, and Jesus for allowing her to do it (Luke 7). It was Pharisees who brought to Jesus the woman who had committed adultery. Even allowing for the gospel writers being prejudiced against the Pharisees, they seem to have presented a very judgemental and condemning image!

It may well have been the Pharisees whom Jesus had in mind when he poked fun at what he called "this generation" and its negative mindset. It was impossible to make any headway with people who were determined to pick holes in everything:

> "To what can I compare this generation? They are like children sitting in the market-places and calling out to others:
> 'We played the flute for you and you did not dance;
> We sang a dirge for you and you did not mourn.'
> For John came neither eating nor drinking, and they say, 'He has a demon.'
> The Son of Man came eating and drinking, and they say, 'Here is a glutton and a drunkard, a friend of tax collectors and sinners.'"
>
> (Matthew 11 v 16–10)

Jesus, of course, was well able to be condemning when he needed to be – witness the famous incident when he ejected the money changers and livestock merchants from the temple. But on the whole, he seems to have avoided being judgemental. The apostle John states clearly that condemnation was not part of Jesus' mission:

> "For God did not send his Son into the world to condemn the world, but to save the world through him." (John 3 v 17)

In his teaching, Jesus strongly urged the importance of not passing judgement on others. Again, the Sermon on the Mount illustrates this:

> "Do not judge, or you too will be judged. For in the same way as you judge others, you will be judged, and with the measure you use, it will be measured to you.
> Why do you look at the speck of sawdust in your brother's eye and pay no attention to the plank in your own eye? You hypocrite, first take the plank out of your own eye, and then you will see clearly to remove the speck from your brother's eye.
> (Matthew 7 v 1–5)

What's Jesus saying here? The obvious interpretation is that it is acceptable to remove the speck from your brother's eye, provided you first examine yourself and remove the plank from your own. But a little reflection revels that here is more to this statement than meets the eye. (Forgive the double meaning!)

Jesus is making a point here which is not immediately obvious, partly because some of the significance is lost in translation. What each of us has in our own eye, according to Jesus, is an enormous piece of wood. Some translations call it a beam. It is too heavy to move and so big that it is impossible to see around it. It is a fixture. Removing the beam from your own eye is something you are not capable of doing. Strain as you will you will never lift it, and stretch as you will, you will never succeed in looking round it. It permanently blocks your field of vision.

Jesus is not saying, "Remove the beam from your eye before you criticise the other person." He is saying, "Don't criticise the other person at all, because you have a beam permanently blocking your own vision which makes it likely that you will do more harm than good by trying to remove the speck from their eye." Our inability to judge with clear, unhindered vision is a major reason for avoiding condemnation of other people. And that's the real point of what Jesus is saying. None of us ever does reach the point where we are so free from error that we can see clearly enough to properly correct others.

Another good reason is the fact that God guarantees that the standards we apply to others are the ones God will use to judge us:

> "But I tell you that everyone will have to give account on the day of judgement for every careless word they have spoken. For by your words you will be acquitted, and by your words you will be condemned." (Matthew 12 v 36–37)

Statements like this struck at the heart of the Pharisees' normal way of responding to other peoples' sin and failure and must have made them feel uncomfortable. More than once, incidents occurred where Jesus' praise and the Pharisees' condemnation met in a head-on collision. One such occasion, recorded by Luke, was an encounter which took place at the home of a Pharisee called Simon, where Jesus was attending a dinner party. A woman interrupted the gathering who was known to have lived a sinful life. She entered the room where the meal was taking place, carrying a large, alabaster container of expensive, perfumed ointment. The guests would have been reclining on couches around a low table, as was the custom of the time. The woman approached Jesus and stood behind him, at his feet. As she started to speak to him, explaining the reason for her presence, she was overcome with emotion and began to cry. As she did so, some of her tears fell on Jesus' feet. In what was probably an immediate, unpremeditated response of embarrassment and apology she swiftly knelt down and wiped the tears off with the nearest suitable material she could find – her own hair. Still acting impulsively, she then began to kiss Jesus' feet, repeatedly. Finally, she broke open the jar and poured the perfume onto Jesus' feet.

In view of the woman's notoriety, Simon, the host, might have expected Jesus to pull away from her and order her to leave. But Simon was horrified to find Jesus doing the opposite. He allowed her to continue kissing his feet, without stopping her – imagine what the *papparazzi* and the gutter press would make of a photo-opportunity like this today! Jesus even raised no objection to the dramatic gesture of pouring the perfume over his feet. The woman's action of wiping her tears from his feet, then kissing his feet and anointing them, was probably a spontaneous expression of gratitude and affection. But it had obviously erotic overtones for anyone who wanted to interpret the situation in that way. These would have been exaggerated in Simon's mind by his knowledge of the woman's past history. The "sin" to which Simon refers is more likely to be sexual sin than anything else. Simon's private reaction, of which Jesus is aware, is one of horror. "If this man really were a prophet," he thinks, "He would know who is touching him and what kind of woman she is – that she is a sinner."

But Jesus began to talk to Simon about forgiveness and the gratitude which flows from it. Jesus' concluding comments here are interesting:

> "Therefore, I tell you, her many sins have been forgiven – for she loved much. But he who has been forgiven little, loves little."
> (Luke 7 v 47, New International Version, 1984 edition)

With his critical, condemning, Pharisee attitude, Simon knew little about forgiveness. The woman knew she had sinned grossly. This was not the first time she had experienced rejection and hostility from other people because of her sinfulness. I imagine she was ashamed and hated herself and what she had done. To her, being told she was forgiven brought an overwhelming sense of gratitude and joy.

But Jesus said she was forgiven because she loved much. What does that mean? It might mean simply that she was forgiven because of the deep love for Jesus and for God which she had discovered. But there is also the shade of a possibility that her sins had been motivated, at least in part, by love and compassion for other people. Could it be that Jesus realised this and was drawing attention to it? The 2011 edition of the New International Version changed the wording of this passage to say "as her great love has shown." Presumably this change was made to rule out any suggestion that Jesus was making excuses for the woman. But the wording of the 1984 version accurately reflects the wording of the Greek. Just think for a moment of how it might have come about that this woman was drawn into sin – how indeed many other people, year by year, wake up to find that they have crossed the line between righteousness and wrongdoing. Her emotional response to Jesus suggests that she was a warm hearted, compassionate person. Perhaps her loving, compassionate nature had led her into a caring relationship with a man in need. Perhaps, drawn by sympathy and admiration, she had begun to give him love that was not hers to give or his to receive? Then, swept away by passion, she found she had stepped over the line and was now an adulteress.

I'm not saying it was like that – but it could have been. It is a trap many people have fallen into. A caring, warm hearted person offers comfort and a listening ear to a fellow human being in pain and provides quite literally a shoulder to cry on. They take the hurting person in their embrace and provide comfort and encouragement. But then proximity brings arousal, gratitude produces affection, and the situation escalates. It is an all too familiar story. Perhaps it was hers. Maybe there had been a string of such situations in her life – hurt and weary men had told their stories to her compassionate listening ear. Her arms had reached out spontaneously in tender, motherly concern to provide comfort. Perhaps unscrupulous men had taken advantage of her tender heart and her trusting nature.

This may not have been how this woman fell into sin but it could have been and, if it was, Jesus' words indicate that he saw beyond the infringement of the law code to the heart of compassion and love which had been the woman's motivation. He contrasts her warm heart with the condemning outlook of the Pharisee, and says she is forgiven because, although she sinned, she did it out of a motive of love. Simon, on the other hand, was condemned because, although he had not sinned, his heart was critical and unloving.

There are strong similarities between this encounter and the even more powerful account of Jesus with the adulterous woman recorded in John, chapter 8. Again, the Pharisees bring the woman to Jesus, admittedly to test him. They may have suspected, on the basis of earlier incidents such as the one at Simon's house, that Jesus would take a lenient attitude towards her. If he did, they could accuse him of condoning adultery and contradicting the law of Moses. Under the Old Testament law, the penalty for adultery was stoning to death. However, Roman law overruled Jewish law because Judaea was a Roman province and the Romans did not allow the Jews to conduct their own executions. So, if Jesus did come down on the side of having the woman stoned to death, they would be able to accuse him to the Romans for inciting disobedience to Roman rule. This was another of those situations where the Pharisees tried to drive Jesus into a corner. However, the Pharisees would have been in no doubt about one thing. The woman had sinned and deserved to be punished. The right thing to do, according to the Old Testament, was to stone the woman to death. That was the penalty the law of Moses demanded and they would have wanted to uphold the law. They were not bringing the woman in the hope that Jesus would let them off the hook and say, "It's alright, you don't need to subject her to such a terrible punishment." Their attitude to her was hostile and condemning. They were actively hoping that Jesus would give them the go ahead to stone her because that's what they thought she deserved.

Preachers sometimes draw attention to the absence of the woman's co-offender in the adultery. The Old Testament law required that the two should be stoned together – she had been caught in the act of adultery so the man was there too when she was caught – but where was he now? The Pharisees have brought the woman to Jesus but not the man.

Perhaps they were going along with a socially conditioned assumption that the woman was to blame – her seductive powers had led the man astray. We see things differently today, of course. Feminism has exploded the myth of women's dangerous seductive powers that men have so often used as a lame excuse for their own weakness. Today, it might well be the man who was exposed and the woman who was left alone, labelled perhaps as a victim of the man's physical or persuasive power.

There is no way we can know the real situation of this woman. She might have been a devious seductress or a prostitute. She might have been a victim of sexual abuse or one half of an illicit love-affair. We don't know if she was guilty and, if she was, whether she was repentant. All we know is that the Pharisees laid the blame fully and squarely on her.

Today, as always, even when offenders in sexual or other sins are genuinely repentant, there will be Pharisees around who will want to make an example of them, to make a clear statement that immoral, selfish, destructive and sinful behaviour cannot be tolerated. But Jesus' response is very different. His answer, "If any one of you is without sin, let him be the first to throw a stone at her," is famous, stunning in its wisdom and absolute rightness. But it is what Jesus said when the group of Pharisees had dispersed and left the woman alone with him and the crowd of onlookers which is most important:

> "Then neither do I condemn you. Go, now and leave your life of sin." (John 8 v 11)

This incident appears in the Bible at the beginning of chapter 8 of John's gospel. However, the earliest manuscripts omit it or place it elsewhere. Because of this, scholars usually conclude that it was not part of John's gospel as originally written. This is a separate, isolated anecdote about Jesus, which somehow managed to get inserted into John's gospel by a scribe who was copying it at a later date. Nevertheless, there is a clear link to the verses that follow on from the point in the gospel where it was inserted. Again, the Pharisees are pointing the finger of accusation:

> "Here you are, appearing as your own witness; your testimony is not valid." (John 8 v 13)

In his response to this accusation, Jesus again takes up the issue of judging:

> "You judge by human standards ..." (John 8 v 15)

Put yourself in the position of one of the Pharisees, hearing Jesus say this for the first time and not knowing what Jesus is going to say next. "You judge by human standards ..." Jesus begins. How would you expect him to complete the sentence? What is going to come next?

The obvious follow-on is, "... but I judge from God's point of view?" We expect Jesus to say, "I have information and insight which you don't. My judgement is sharper, more accurate and reliable than yours. My judgement is superior and true." But he says nothing of the kind. He simply states,

> "...I pass judgement on no one." (John 8 v 15)

Stop and think about that. It is important. Jesus doesn't judge anyone. Admittedly he goes on to say " if I do, my decisions are right, because I am not alone. I stand with the Father, who sent me." But the important part is what comes first. Jesus says, "I pass judgement on no-one". He didn't and he doesn't. One day he will. God has set a day when mankind will be judged and he has placed responsibility for executing that judgement in the hands of Jesus, as Jesus himself said, in words recorded in John 5 v 25–30:

> "Very truly I tell you, a time is coming and has now come when the dead will hear the voice of the Son of God and those who hear will live. For as the Father has life in himself, so he has granted the Son to have life in himself. And he has given him authority to judge because he is the Son of Man.
>
> "Do not be amazed at this, for a time is coming when all who are in the graves will hear his voice and come out – those who have done good will rise and live and those who have done evil will rise to be condemned. By myself I can do nothing; I judge only as I hear and my judgement is just, for I seek not to please myself but him who sent me."
>
> (John 15 v 25–30)

There will be a day of judgement, and Jesus will be the judge. But that day has not yet come. Jesus, God's judge to be, held back from passing sentence on the adulterous woman, because the time for judgement had not yet come. The Pharisees were in error in their eagerness to condemn those who sinned. God had not appointed them as judge over their fellow men. They were the wrong people to judge and it was the wrong time to pass judgement. The same, of course, holds true for us.

The One who is one day to judge mankind refrained, most of the time, from condemning others. But those who did condemn their fellow human beings got the sharp end of his tongue. At the same time he was beautifully, refreshingly free with his praise. Here are some examples:

> "Daughter, your faith has healed you." (Mark 5 v 34)
>
> "For such a reply, you may go." (Mark 7 v 29)
>
> "Leave her alone. Why are you bothering her? She has done a beautiful thing for me..." (Mark 14 v 6)
>
> "Blessed are you, Simon son of Jonah, for this was not revealed to you by man but by my Father in heaven." (Matthew 16 v 17)
>
> "I tell you the truth, I have not found anyone in Israel with such great faith …" (Matthew 8 v 10)
>
> "Mary has chosen what is better" (Luke 10 v 42)
>
> "All these people gave their gifts out of their wealth; but she out of her poverty put in all she had to live on." (Luke 21 v 4)
>
> "Leave her alone ... it was intended that she should save this perfume for the day of my burial. (John 12 v 7)
>
> "Today you will be with me in paradise." (Luke 23 v 43)

Chapter five

Guilt by Association

"Why does your teacher eat with tax collectors and sinners?"
(Matthew 9 v 11)

It was a typical Pharisee question: critical and condemning as always! To the Pharisees there were only two kinds of people: good ones who kept the law and bad people who didn't. They thought it was essential to maintain a clear distinction between the two. Righteous people had to be condemned and good people had to be praised. Disapproval and praise went hand in hand. The disapproval they gave to lawbreakers had the spin-off of earning them credit for keeping the law themselves – there was a certain amount of self interest in the Pharisees' stand for righteousness!

One way to show your disapproval towards lawbreakers was to withdraw from them. They regarded people who did consort with known sinners as being guilty by association. They assumed that people who met with those people socially were condoning their wrong behaviour.

The same attitude is around today, both in society as a whole and, regrettably, among Christians. This approach often motivates the popular press who see everything in black and white, so that it only takes one small indiscretion on the part of a public figure for a hundred acts of public service and generosity to be overlooked. Even among Christians you'd better beware of getting too close to people who are immoral, or even those who have the "wrong" theological outlook, or who embrace some unorthodox doctrine. If you do, you can be sure that the rumour will get about that you are the same as them! If you are an Evangelical, make sure you aren't seen on the same platform as a Catholic or a Liberal, because people will see it as condoning their "false" doctrine! If you are a Liberal, don't show your face at a Charismatic conference, or you might lose your credibility as a balanced and thinking person!

Jesus' approach was very different, as revealed by His response when he heard about the question the Pharisees had put to his disciples:

> "It is not the healthy who need a doctor, but those who are ill. But go and learn what this means: 'I desire mercy, not sacrifice. For I have not come to call the righteous, but sinners.' "
>
> (Matthew 9 v 13)

Jesus' approach to lawbreakers was to get alongside them and build a relationship. He took pains to get to know them and through his love and kindness to earn the permission to speak into their lives. He saw them, not as sinners needing punishment, but as sick people who needed healing. That doesn't mean that he condoned the things they did – by no means! As we have already seen, he made a clear statement of his understanding of right and wrong in the Sermon on the Mount. He spoke clearly and forcefully about the judgement to come, about the danger of being shut out of God's kingdom, banished to the darkness outside or burned up by fires of remorse in God's equivalent of the Jerusalem refuse-tip. But he knew that by withdrawing from sinners he would deprive them of the opportunity of being challenged and corrected by his words and influenced and shamed into righteousness by the purity of his character. God hadn't sent him to earth to give good people a pat on the back. God had sent him to rescue sinners and there was no way he could do that without meeting some! Jesus' followers today share in the same mission, so the same applies to us, too.

The Pharisees should have been familiar with the writings of one of the prophets, Hosea, who had lived about 800 years earlier. Like many of the prophets, Hosea lived his message as well as speaking it, but in so doing, he posed the Pharisees a problem. They apparently hadn't noticed the problem until Jesus drew their attention to it. The problem was that God told Hosea to marry an adulteress.

There is some uncertainty about the details of the story. It may be that Gomer was unfaithful to Hosea after marrying him, leaving him in order to consort with another man and Hosea divorced her because of this, but later took her back as his wife again. In that case, Hosea went against the law because Deuteronomy 24 v 1–4 forbids a man who has divorced in those circumstances to take his wife back.

However, the text can be taken to mean that, when Hosea married Gomer in the first place, she was already an adulteress, who had left her first husband or been divorced by him, and was now working as a prostitute (see Hosea chapter 1 v 2 to chapter 3 v 2). If this was the case, by marrying Gomer and having children by her, Hosea broke God's law, even though he was acting at God's command. Gomer should already have been stoned to death anyway, and, since she was divorced, Hosea should not have married her, as Jesus himself said in Luke 16 v 18. Either way, Hosea was breaking the Law of God – yet he claimed that God had told him to do it.

Picture a scene: a man comes to the pastor or vicar of your church and says, "God told me to get married to this lady whose last husband divorced her because she works as a prostitute – and I wondered if you would do the wedding?" How many pastors would even consult with their fellow elders or their bishop to weigh the message and decide if it was from God or not? This is the kind of "prophecy" that makes pastors hit the roof with panic and disapproval!

But that's what God said. And that's what Hosea did. According to the Pharisees, he shouldn't even have walked on the same side of the street as Gomer, let alone shared a bed with her! Was Hosea deceived? Was he suffering from a psychotic illness with religious delusions? No way! God really said that to him and he was obedient. God had a reason. He was giving Hosea a message to communicate. The message was that Israel was like Gomer – an unfaithful, immoral, disloyal wife.

Israel couldn't stay true to God for one minute. Israelites were ignoring God and continually worshipping gods of all the other nations around them. And, yes, he would have to judge them. But one thing he would never do was divorce them. No matter how badly they sinned against him, mercy was always going to be to the fore in his response. He had married himself to Israel in mercy. The nation had not been faithful to him, even at the start. They didn't deserve to be the chosen people. But God had "married" himself to them in full knowledge of their national character. Like Hosea, God knew what he was getting. The people of Israel continued to turn away from God time and time again, but always God was prepared to show mercy when they repented and to take them back. God chose Hosea to act out in his own life the mercy and patience God showed to his adulterous bride, Israel, as he pleaded with them to return to their Maker and Husband.

Why am I talking about Hosea? Well, it was in the context of Hosea's prophecies that God said to Israel:

> "I desire mercy, not sacrifice, and acknowledgement of God rather than burnt offerings." (Hosea 6 v 6)

– the very words Jesus quoted to the Pharisees. 800 years before Jesus quoted Hosea's words, God had told his people through Hosea that outward observance of laws and rituals was not enough. God was looking for something that came from the heart. Hosea didn't reject Gomer because of her sin, but tried to melt her and win her love through the mercy he showed to her. In the same way God was showing mercy to Israel, wanting to win her with his love. He wanted his people to respond first with a heart acknowledgement of God, to return love for love. Secondly he wanted them to show to others the mercy he had shown them. This was more important than the sacrifices and offerings and observance of the Law, though these had their place as expressions of their heart response.

The Pharisees were certainly not showing mercy and, though outwardly they kept the law, it is doubtful whether many of them actually honoured and loved God from the heart in the way that Hosea described. They didn't understand God's heart of mercy towards his people, and were actually working against God in their enthusiasm to condemn sinners.

The conversion of Zacchaeus, the tax collector, recorded in Luke chapter 15, gives a powerful illustration of what Jesus was seeking to achieve. When Jesus invited himself to a meal at Zacchaeus' house, Luke tells us, people began to mutter: "He has gone to be a guest at the house of a sinner." Zacchaeus had got rich as a tax farmer, extorting large amounts of money from the poor and passing on what was due to the Roman Government, while pocketing as much as he could get away with for himself.

But somehow, during the course of a brief meeting with Jesus, Zacchaeus' life and values were turned inside out and upside down (as were his pockets!) His repentance was immediate and thorough: "Look, Lord! Here and now I give half of my possessions to the poor and, if I have cheated anybody out of anything, I will pay back four times the amount." (Luke 19 v 8)

As Jesus said, salvation had come to his house. "For the son of Man came to seek and to save what was lost." (Luke 19 v 10). The Pharisees had only one remedy for those who were lost. That was for them to stay lost – to stay outside the community, to wait until the day of judgement when they would get their just desserts from God. But Jesus had something better to offer.

In Chapter 15 of his gospel, Luke records another occasion when the Pharisees levelled the same criticism at Jesus: "This fellow welcomes sinners and eats with them." On this occasion Jesus responded by telling three stories, all of which illustrate God's passion to win back those who have strayed away from him – the parables of the Lost Sheep, The Lost Coin and the Lost Son. These three parables, more than any other passages in the New Testament, reveal the heart of Jesus' understanding of God and the motivation for his own ministry. And, since Jesus is God incarnate, these parables also reveal God's heart. A lot is said about "man's search for God" but these passages reveal that in fact, it is God who is looking for us.

Some theologians have suggested that these parables illustrate a unique element in Jesus' teaching which had not been part of Jewish thought before – the idea of God as the Divine Shepherd, not waiting for people to turn to him but actively seeking them. However, this thought was not new to Jesus. There is a great deal in the Old Testament about God as shepherd and the idea of sinners as wayward sheep is clearly present in Isaiah 53 v 6,

> "We all, like sheep, have gone astray, each of us has turned to his own way…"

What is new in Jesus is not that he portrayed God as a shepherd, but that as God he was willing to become a sacrificial lamb. He took on the role of the suffering servant described in the same chapter, willing to be not only the shepherd looking for his sheep, but the Lamb that was killed in their place:

> "... and the Lord has laid on him the iniquity of us all."
> (Isaiah 53 v 6)

> "He was led like a lamb to the slaughter, and as a sheep before her shearers is silent, so he did not open his mouth."
> (Isaiah 53 v 7)

There are a number of reasons why people fall into sin or turn their backs on God.

Foolishness

Sometimes it is through their own foolishness. Like the lost sheep, they turn a deaf ear to the Shepherd's voice. They reach out a little further and a little further after something they find attractive or desirable and suddenly find themselves in a mess, with a trail of damage behind them, or imprisoned and unable to extricate themselves from a situation they brought on themselves by their own folly. In those situations, God comes after us. He hears our cry, forgives and acts to rescue us and, because Jesus was willing as the sinless Son of God to die in our place, God can forgive our sins. The Pharisees didn't believe that Jesus was the Son of God, and they didn't know that his death, which they were plotting to bring about, was going to be the means of salvation for sinners. If someone had explained it to them, would their attitude to Jesus have been any different? Perhaps they would have been horrified at the idea that God could spare those who failed to keep the Law? Some of them certainly were, when the early Christians began to publicise the message.

There were even Christians who found this difficult to come to terms with, as revealed by the asides in Paul's letter to the Christians in Rome:

> "What shall we say then ? Shall we go on sinning, so that grace may increase?"
>
> "What then, shall we sin because we are not under the law but under grace?" (Romans 6 v 1, 15)

"If sins can be forgiven, why bother to be good?" was the short-sighted response of people with a pharisaical outlook. But the right motive for goodness is not avoiding judgement; it is enjoying God's presence and his love. Obedience which arises out of fear of punishment is dishonouring to a loving God. But the Pharisees hadn't worked that one out yet. And many people still haven't.

Grief

There are some people who go astray from God as a result of things which they suppose God has done to them. They have lost a loved one, experienced some terrible tragedy. In their anguish they close their hearts to God, unable to believe or trust his love any longer. Or maybe, in God's providence, they are brought up in a situation where they do not hear about God or are misinformed about him so that they go through life without being properly told about him. These people are like the coin that the woman lost. Like the woman in the parable, God engages in a thorough search, leaving no stone unturned until he establishes contact with them.

Whether people are lost through foolishness or the circumstances of life, God's response when they return is the same:

> "...there will be more rejoicing in heaven over one sinner who

> repents than over ninety-nine righteous people who do not need to repent." (Luke 15 v 7)

Rebellion

There is, finally, a third reason why people lose contact with God. The story of the Lost Son deals with that that one. There are some people who simply rebel against God. They know who he is and are aware of his love, yet they still turn away from him to live life their own way. They treat the very goodness and generosity of God with contempt and squander the gifts they know he has given them. When we are in this situation we have no excuse. We can't plead ignorance, and can't hide behind the excuses of weakness, or folly. The Pharisees assumed that, for people like this, there was no forgiveness. No atonement could be made for deliberate and calculated sin. Such people do not deserve to be forgiven.

Yet, as Jesus showed through the parable, it makes no difference to God whether a person deserves forgiveness or not. In any case, "deserving forgiveness" is a contradiction in terms. If you need forgiveness, by definition you do not deserve it. The fact that you need to be forgiven assumes that you have sinned and deserve to be condemned.

The son came to his senses and returned to his father but he did not deserve to come back home as a son. He came asking for a job. But the father, who represents God, was longing for him to return and was looking out for him. For the father in the story, who the son was, was more important than what he had done. Maintaining the relationship was more important than fulfiling the demands of justice. So it is with God. God has given us laws to enable us to maintain good relationships with him and with one another. But God is more concerned with relationships being healed and maintained than he is with laws being kept and punishment being meted out, shocking though this was (and is) for Pharisees to discover.

In an incredible display of mercy, the father lavishes love and welcome on the returning son who has sinned against him so grievously, but has now come to his senses. He takes off the son's old, worn-out and travel-stained clothes and replaces them with garments which symbolise status and authority, and he throws a party to welcome him home.

Jesus' message is very clear: God's love and forgiveness are available even for those whose sin has been deliberate and thorough – provided they come to their senses and are prepared to repent. More than that, God positively delights to welcome such people. Furthermore, repentance is not, as the Pharisees might have supposed, just a matter of correcting wrong behaviour – it is returning to a right relationship with God.

However, the story doesn't end with the prodigal's return. As has often been pointed out, the story is as much about the reactions of the elder son as it is about the love of the father. Remember the reason Jesus told these three stories? It began with the accusation of the Pharisees: "This man welcomes sinners and eats with them." The elder brother in the story shares the same attitude as the Pharisees. They would have identified very readily with his response, but would no doubt have felt shamed by the way Jesus reflected their own hardness of heart in the elder brother's attitude.

The return of the prodigal, and the love and mercy that the father lavished on him, created a crisis for the elder brother. His reaction is understandable. He had been an exemplary son. He had been patient, willing to wait until his father's death before receiving his inheritance. He had worked hard and long for his father all the years that the younger son had been away. He had felt taken for granted by his father, perhaps. To see his wasteful, irresponsible younger brother being fêted and affirmed and receiving tokens of love and acceptance from their father provokes intense jealousy. No wonder he is annoyed!

The truth is that the elder brother was no less loved and appreciated by the father. "My son," the father says, "You are always with me, and everything I have is yours." The elder brother could have had new clothes, a party, a fatted calf, any time he wanted to. He only had to ask. The younger son asked in faith and received, even though he was unworthy. The elder brother, who had some claim to worthiness, tried to earn the father's love (which he didn't need to earn, because it was there anyway) and failed to experience it, because he never had the faith to ask for anything. He got it wrong, just as much as his younger brother. The key to the father's love and acceptance was faith, love and repentance – not hard work and effort to make himself acceptable. The younger son thought that his father couldn't possibly love him after what he had done. The elder son thought the father must surely love him, since his behaviour was so exemplary. Both were mistaken. The father loved both his sons for one reason and one reason only – because they were his. The younger son's irresponsible behaviour couldn't destroy that love and the elder son's solid reliability couldn't add to it.

The prodigal son, in fact, experienced more of his father's love than the older brother because he trusted his father's goodness and wasn't afraid to ask. True, he should not have wasted the inheritance, but in that one important respect he outshone the older brother who held back. In the same way, none of us can earn God's love. He loves us because we are his – for no other reason. He gives because we trust his promises and ask in faith, not because we deserve anything he gives us.

The elder brother in Jesus' story very obviously represents the Pharisees. However, in telling the story, Jesus was not simply making fun of them or even just pointing out that their view of God was wrong. He was holding out an invitation and a promise to them. He was inviting them, with the elder brother, to come and join the party. Through the words of the father in the story he pleaded with them not only to come and join in celebrating the repentance of others who had sinned, but also to come into a full heart-knowledge of the Father's real love for them. Jesus felt anger at the distortion of God's real character which the Pharisees were perpetrating, but he also felt compassion for these "elder brothers" who were exercising so much discipline and effort to earn the approval and acceptance God wanted to give them for free. They were experiencing neither the pleasures of the far country nor the joy of the Father's mercy. They would have felt intense jealousy for anyone who managed to take in both, and this imprisoned them in resentment and righteous indignation, so that they were unable to experience, or share, their Father's joy.

it is easy for us to look back and condemn the Pharisees for their attitude towards sinners, but the same attitudes are common today, both among Christians and in the wider community. Many people believe that the church is there to protect and promote standards of right and wrong, at least among private individuals (there is always an outcry if corporate morality is brought into the question and some church leader criticises the morality of government policies!) The press pour scorn on the church for its hypocrisy and then themselves hypocritically take on the church's traditional role, seeking out wrong doing and exposing it to public disdain in "exclusive" articles. The public attitude seems to be that people who do wrong should pay for it, and respectable law abiding citizens should keep a distance from wrongdoers to make a clear statement of public disapproval. How badly the church has failed in its task of communicating the gospel if this parody of Christian belief is so widely accepted as what the church ought to stand for!

Unfortunately, the popular attitude has been carried over unthinkingly into church life by many who regard themselves as Christians. People see the task of the church as protest, rather than proclamation. Christians give their time, not to communicating the message of the coming judgement and God's offer of mercy, but to communicating their disapproval of the ills of society and the sins of others. All too often it never occurs to them to actually make contact with those who are responsible for those ills. Yet it is only by engaging people in discussion, finding out what motivates them, showing them the love of Jesus and reasoning with them about a better way that we can effectively change their behaviour. Society sees Christians as a condemning bunch of people who shout disapproval from a safe distance – as Pharisees, in effect.

However this was not Jesus' way. And if we are going to be faithful to our Master, we have to learn to tackle sinners the way he did. That means we begin by getting to know them, understanding them and loving them where they are, in order to prescribe the right application of the grace of God. When we have won their trust and communicated the love of God to them, then we can begin to question their belief structures and point them to the truth revealed in Jesus. Once they know the truth they will condemn themselves – we won't need to do it for them. Our privilege will then be to point them to the grace of God revealed in his Son who has paid the price for them to be forgiven and restored to fellowship with God as their Father.

Chapter six

Good God!

The grace of God – that was the central point at issue between Jesus and the Pharisees.

He and they were both zealously devoted to God. They called God by the same name – but in fact they worshipped different gods. Or at least, the Pharisees' idea of God differed widely from the God Jesus came to reveal. You can see the difference clearly in Luke's account of how Jesus healed the paralysed man who was let down through the roof by his friends. We have already looked at Matthew's version of this incident (see chapter 3, "Why be Good Anyway?"). But Mark and Luke show a slightly different slant in their accounts of what happened. After Jesus said to the man, "Friend, your sins are forgiven," Luke reports,

> "The Pharisees and the Teachers of the Law began thinking among themselves, 'Who is this fellow who speaks blasphemy? *Who can forgive sins but God alone?'*"
>
> (Luke 5 v. 21, emphasis mine)

There is a bias in the words in italics which is not immediately obvious. The Pharisees were not simply saying that only God can forgive sins. They were going beyond that. Their assumption was that God is the only person who can forgive sins a*nd that he is unlikely to do so.* If they believed that God forgave sins readily, they would not have been so shocked by what Jesus said. They would have understood Jesus as saying, "Never mind friend; God is merciful; he always forgives. Your sins are forgiven too." If they believed that God was quick to forgive, they would have assumed that Jesus was simply reassuring the man of the forgiveness he could expect from a gracious God. Forgiveness holds no surprises for those who know God to be merciful. Their shock and disapproval came partly because Jesus appeared to be usurping God's position in forgiving the man's sins, but more importantly because, according to their thinking, God was not quick to forgive. They reasoned, "God is holy; he punishes sin, because he is just. This man is suffering because he has done something wrong and God is punishing him for it. This paralysis is God's judgement on him." They saw Jesus' words as a double blasphemy. He was both usurping God's position and, in their view, misrepresenting him.

The same applies to the passages where Jesus healed people on the Sabbath. As Jesus pointed out to the Pharisees (Matthew 12 v 11) even a Pharisee would go to the rescue of a sheep that had fallen into a pit on the Sabbath. Yet they assumed that the Sabbath law would prevent God going to the rescue of people in need. In other words, they believed God was even less compassionate than they were.

But Jesus stood before them representing the God who had established laws to make sure his people enjoyed peace and spiritual and physical health. Jesus was not going to allow anyone to use those laws to imprison people in sickness, disharmony and spiritual danger. He represented the God who had both the power and the will to forgive repentant sinners. More than that, Jesus represented the God who delegates his authority in such a way that he not only authorises his Son to forgive sins, he even commissions his Son's followers to do so too (see John 20 v. 21).

The God Jesus revealed is good and generous. Righteous, holy and just, yes, but also overflowing with mercy, compassion and love. Luke's three parables of the lost things, which we examined in the last chapter, illustrate this perfectly, in particular the Parable of the Prodigal Son. As we saw, the interaction between the elder brother and the father in this story is crucially important. In the elder brother's mind, the prodigal son should have been punished and should have remained permanently in a state of deprivation as a reminder of his disloyalty to his father. Fortunately for the prodigal, the father was a loving, compassionate man, and in this he was a fitting representative of God. Jesus came to reveal a God who does forgive sins, who does act in compassion, and who, though he has real authority and power, does not hold it to himself but is willing to delegate it through others whom he calls to share in his work.

In a similar way, many of the disputes which take place in the church today boil down, in essence, to a disagreement about the character of God. Is he a Calvinist God – unyielding, uncompromising, and totally in control, or is he an Arminian God who has abandoned the world and "gone fishing" until Judgement Day? Is he a Charismatic God, who delights to talk to His children, have fun with them, give them gifts and even make them laugh, or is he the stern, disapproving, detached judge who was feared by an earlier generation of Christians? Many disagreements between Christians can be readily solved when we take them back to the essential questions: "What kind of God are we dealing with?" and "What is his character and personality?"

To answer that question we have to go to Jesus. "He that has seen me has seen the Father," Jesus said. Jesus' understanding of God was fully in tune with the Old Testament, including the books of the Law. The popular view that there is a vengeful, cruel, God of the Old Testament as distinct from the kind, loving God presented in the New Testament is far from true. There is no difference between the God revealed in the Law and the God revealed by Jesus. God declared himself to Moses as:

> "… compassionate and gracious, slow to anger, abounding in love and faithfulness, maintaining love to thousands and forgiving wickedness, rebellion and sin." (Exodus 34 v 6 and 7).

Jesus revealed God in his life in exactly the same terms as God had revealed himself in the Law of Moses.

It's all too easy to impose onto God an image of what you think He should be like, or even what you fear he may be like. Some of us, in effect, create God in our own image. Some people imagine God in the image of their father or the authority figures they have encountered in their life. But we need to keep going back to the God Jesus revealed. It is very easy to err on the side of making God out to be more severe than he really is. Many people do that and, in doing so, take the side of the Pharisees. It is more difficult, though possible, to make God out to be more easy-going and permissive than he is. To do either you have to overlook the way Jesus died and the reason for His death. The sacrifice of an only Son has to indicate the deepest and most amazing compassion. How amazing that God would go even to the length of allowing his Son to suffer a slow and incredibly painful death to make it possible for us to be forgiven and restored to fellowship with him! This is not a God who is detached and uncaring, or unforgiving. At the same time, in the cross, there is a reminder of the seriousness with which God views sin. By forgiving us, God is not implying that sin does not matter. The suffering and death of his Son are the sign that it does matter. In the cross, though, mercy triumphs over judgement. God's goodness triumphs over his righteousness, or rather the two are combined in a new definition of what real righteuosness is.

Jesus knew God. It is difficult for us to know just what this meant for him in his incarnation. Could he remember his pre-existent life in relationship with the Father and the Spirit? Maybe so. At the very least he knew His Father from the Old Testament scriptures and through his life of prayer. He also had an awareness that he was one with the Father and the Spirit and that their character was his character. In the end we can't really understand what it meant for him. Theologians have wondered about it for centuries and the only really honest answer is that we don't know. We know enough to make theological definitions, but not to understand exactly what it was like for Jesus. However, Jesus certainly had a closeness of relationship with God that exceeded anything we experience. He knew God as no-one else has ever done.

There is only one thing that makes a person more indignant than having their own character misrepresented, and that is having someone misrepresent the character of someone else they know and love very dearly. Perhaps that's why Jesus got so indignant with the Pharisees. As far as he was concerned, they were doing both. They were doing him an injustice but worse, they were also misrepresenting his Father.

God is good – Jesus knew it. The Pharisees hadn't quite grasped how kind God really is. Neither have we. But the closer we get to Jesus, the more overwhelming his kindness becomes.

Chapter seven

Letter and Spirit

We have noted so far that Jesus differed from the Pharisees on five issues:

1. The nature of goodness
For Jesus, goodness is to do with the motivation of the heart and will. For the Pharisees it is to do with keeping rules.

2. Motives for goodness
For Jesus, goodness is an expression of our love for God and others. For the Pharisees, it is a way to obtain love from God and others.

3. Condemnation and praise
Jesus emphasised mercy and rewards for goodness, while also warning of the judgement to come.
The Pharisees emphasised condemnation and blame.

4. Their attitude to sinners
Jesus sought out the company of sinners in order to challenge and influence them.
The Pharisees dissociated themselves from sinners and avoided their company.

5. The character of God

Jesus described and demonstrated the generosity, mercy and compassion of God, along with his justice.
The Pharisees portrayed God as eager to find fault and thorough in his condemnation of sin and sinners.

There is one further difference between Jesus and the Pharisees for us to add to the list.

6. Why the Old Testament law was given and what it aimed to achieve.

We have already seen that Jesus summarised God's law in the two great commandments, "Love the Lord your God with all your heart, soul and strength" and "Love your neighbour as yourself". Both of these foundational commandments are concerned with relationships – our relationship with God first and then our relationships with one another. The subject of relationships makes up an enormous proportion of Jesus' teaching. Supremely, Jesus was concerned with God's relationship to us and ours with him but he also taught that our relationships with others flow from our relationship with God. Our love for other human beings is an expression of our love for God.

Jesus taught that fellow disciples are to see each other as brothers and sisters, sharing the same father, and should relate to each other accordingly. This comes out strongly in the Sermon on the Mount, where Jesus exhorted his disciples to make peace with brothers they had offended before going to make an offering at the altar, to turn the other cheek and to love even their enemies.

We noted in a previous chapter that Jesus portrayed God as the divine Shepherd who goes looking for a lost sheep and is prepared to make himself a sacrificial lamb in order to bring it back to the fold. God is always seeking relationship with his creatures. Jesus taught that we should imitate God by acting in a similar way towards one another.

Just how much importance Jesus placed on maintaining good relationships is clearly indicated in a key passage in Matthew 18 where Jesus starts by presenting a possible situation in the following words:

"If your brother or sister sins sins against you..." (Matthew 18 v 15) Some of the earliest copies of this passage omit the words "against you", simply saying, "If your brother or sister sins..."

If the longer version is the original one and Jesus said, "if your brother or sister sins against you..." the instructions that follow only apply if a brother or sister has personal personally offended you. If, on the other hand, Jesus simply said, "If your brother or sister sins..." it applies to any situation where a brother or sister has sinned against God or offended anyone else.

The rule of interpretation that translators follow in a situation like this is that the most unlikely reading is the most likely to be original. It is more likely that a scribe would add the words "against you" by way of clarification than that a scribe would omit these words through carelessness. This view is strengthened when we realise that, if Jesus simply said, "If your brother sins...", it would fit with Galatians 6 v 1, where Paul expressed the same teaching:

> "Brothers and sisters, if someone is caught in a sin, you who live by the Spirit should restore that person gently. But watch yourselves or you also may be tempted"

Although the shorter version is more likely to be what Jesus actually said, it isn't certain and either of these two interpretations of the passage is possible, so we should keep both in mind and apply Jesus' teaching practically to both situations, those when we are personally offended or those where the offence is not personal but we see a brother or sister going astray.

In Matthew 18, Jesus advocates a three-stage process to deal with these situations:

1. Make a private approach, on your own, to the fellow Christian who has sinned.
2. If they remain unyielding and obstinate, make a second approach, this time with a witness.
3. If this approach is still unsuccessful, bring the matter to the

church for arbitration. ("The church" here means the whole group of disciples who are in fellowship together).

People often use the words "church discipline" to refer to situations where these instructions are carried out but in reality this is an inappropriate way of describing what Jesus had in mind. The focus is not on discipline but on restoration. "Church maintenance" or "church repair" would be more appropriate ways to describe it. "Discipline" suggests bringing troublemakers into line and enforcing law and order. It brings into the picture threats of rejection and excommunication – "fall into line or else." In contrast, the aim of the process Jesus instituted is not to maintain justice or punish wrongdoers, it is to restore the relationship which has been broken by sin and to make sure that both "brothers" remain in relationship with one another and the church in spite of the offence that has taken place. "If they listen to you," says Jesus, "You have won your brother or sister back."

The popular New International Version translates the last bit as "won them over". This is a disastrous misunderstanding of Jesus' meaning and totally misses the point. The purpose of the exercise is not to gain superiority in an argument but to restore a broken relationship – to regain a brother or sister. If the sinning disciple continues in sin he may cease to be a brother. Even if he hasn't sinned, in the sense of breaking God's law, but continues to act in a way that is unacceptable to a fellow Christian, it will fracture the relationship between them and so divide the church. The aim of Jesus' instructions is to restore the damaged relationship.

All this builds up to an important conclusion: the purpose of the law, for Jesus, is to maintain right relationships. The Ten Commandments are rules to govern relationships. So are all the lesser Old Testament laws. The law is thus not an end in itself but a means to an end, the end being to restore and maintain harmony in human society – peace between man and God, peace between human and human and peace between a person and their own soul. Unless relationships are intact, the law has not been fulfilled. This is why sacrifices and offerings and paying penalties are not enough to fulfil the demands of the law. The law is fulfilled only when repentance, mercy and forgiveness take place and, as a consequence, broken relationships are restored.

For the Pharisees, keeping the law was an end in itself. That meant they could interpret the law and apply it in such a way that, although they fulfilled the letter of the law, the effect was to harm other people and break relationships. People have often observed that the Pharisees were only concerned with keeping the letter of the law, whereas Jesus looked beyond the letter to the spirit and intention behind it.

The Pharisees' emphasis on the letter made it possible for them to exploit loopholes in the law or to avoid keeping one law by bringing another into play. A good example of this is the way they applied the practice of "Corban". Jesus took them to task for this in Matthew 15.

"Corban" was a word that meant "dedicated". Someone could declare part or all of their property as "Corban", meaning it was dedicated to God. This had the effect of leaving it to the Temple in their will. Rather than doing this out of devotion to God, the Pharisees could use it as a way to spite a relative they were angry with, as someone today might write someone out of their will. In a society with no welfare provision the effect could be to condemn relatives and their families to poverty. Everyone had a moral and legal responsibility to look after their parents in old age but the Pharisees allowed people to duck out of this responsibility by declaring their property or savings as "Corban". As Jesus pointed out, this practice contradicted the spirit and intention of the commandment to honour parents.

The Pharisees' approach also led to a short sighted tendency to be preoccupied with the minutiae of the law while overlooking larger issues. Matthew tells us how Jesus brilliantly exposed this in Matthew 23 v. 23:

> "You give a tenth of your spices – mint, dill and cumin. But you have neglected the law – justice, mercy and faithfulness."

The Pharisees were meticulous in tithing even the rows of herbs in their gardens but were ignoring bigger and more important areas of obedience.

The biggest clashes between Jesus and the Pharisees occurred in connection with the commandment not to work on the Sabbath. This was a major issue for the Pharisees. They had worked out elaborate sub clauses for this commandment to specify how heavy a load a person could carry on the Sabbath and how far they could walk on the Sabbath without breaking the law. It was also important to specify precisely when the Sabbath began and ended. If it turned cold on the Sabbath and you lit a fire, was this breaking the commandment? It was important for the Pharisees to know.

Throughout the gospels we find Jesus and the Pharisees coming into conflict repeatedly concerning Sabbath observance. The available evidence suggests that it was because of this issue more than any other that the Pharisees began to seek Jesus' downfall. One reason for this was that, ever since the time of the exile in Babylon, the Sabbath had become an important symbol of Jewish identity. It remained so in the cosmopolitan culture of the Roman empire and still is today. So the Pharisees regarded Jesus as undermining their national identity as well as teaching people to disobey God.

Mark records the beginning of this clash in Mark Chapter 2 v 23 onwards. He describes how Jesus and his disciples were walking through some cornfields on a Sabbath day. As they walked, they began to pluck some ears of corn and to eat them. The commandment said,

> "The seventh day is a Sabbath to the Lord your God. On it you shall not do any work..." (Exodus 20 v 10)

From the point of view of the Pharisees, plucking ears of corn was harvesting and harvesting was work. The disciples were therefore breaking the law.

It is difficult for many of us today to understand the mentality that would regard picking the odd ear of corn as work. To us the Pharisees' approach seems petty – or does it? I'm sure some people reading this will be thinking, "I can see the Pharisees' point." If you are an accountant or a skilled machinist, working in a job that requires scrupulous accuracy with everything carefully boxed and labelled, it can be difficult to stand back and see a bigger picture. Some people see the big picture naturally and have to be nagged into attention to detail. Others only see the brushstrokes and have to be dragged back to a decent distance and have someone say, "Look, there's a picture here!" before they say,"Oh, yes, I think I can see it." The Pharisees had difficulty in seeing the big picture. They only had eyes for the small details. Jesus had broken one of the ten commandments and it caused offence to their tidy, clear-cut system. So they come to him, expressing their disquiet in the form of a question:

> "The Pharisees said to him,"Look, why are they doing what is unlawful on the Sabbath?" (Mark 2 v 24)

When you're faced with a question or criticism, there are usually only a limited number of ways you can respond. So it was with Jesus at this point. If the Pharisees had presented the question to Jesus in a multiple choice format. It would look something like this:

a) Yes, you are right. They are breaking the Law and are wrong to do so. They must stop at once and ask God's forgiveness.

b) No, you've misjudged their actions. They are not breaking the law at all.

c) Sometimes breaking the law is an allowable thing to do and this is one of those occasions. They are justified in breaking the law on this occasion because of particular circumstances which make it allowable.

There are no other possible answers – only these three. So which did Jesus select? It is difficult to be sure at first because he seems to be side-stepping the question. He responded by referring the Pharisees to an incident in the life of King David.

> "Have you never read what David did when he and his companions were hungry and in need? In the days of Abiathar, the high priest, he entered the house of God and ate the consecrated bread, which is lawful only for priests to eat. And he

> also gave some to his companions. (Mark 2 v 25–26)

What is Jesus saying here? He certainly isn't agreeing with the Pharisees – so strike out answer a). But equally, he is not ticking answer b). He isn't saying that the Pharisees have misunderstood the law. So we are left with answer c) – that they were contravening the law but there were special circumstances that made it acceptable for them to do so. But where do David and Abiathar fit into the picture?

The incident Jesus referred to is recorded in I Samuel, chapter 21. David had come to the unwelcome realisation that King Saul was trying to have him killed. As a result, he took a hasty decision to leave the country. In the course of this hurried and stressful journey away from Saul's court, he arrived at a place called Nob, which was where the Holy Tent was pitched at that time. There he met with the High Priest who was called Ahimelech (also known as Abiathar). The Priest asked him why he had come alone and David answered,

> "The King sent me on a mission and said to me 'No-one is to know anything about the mission lam sending you on. As for my men, I have told them to meet me at a certain place." (I Samuel 21 v 2)

Note this carefully: David was telling a lie. King Saul had done no such thing. David was not travelling on a mission from the King, he was running away from him, in fear for his life. One of the ten commandments (number 8) forbids giving false witness. David broke this commandment by lying to the Priest. He then went on to ask the priest to provide some provisions for him and his men. The priest says (in effect), "I'm sorry, David, I don't have anything to give you, other than some consecrated bread which only priests are allowed to eat."

The priest then says he could make an exception for David and his men, provided they are ritually pure – in particular, that none of them had had sexual relationships with any woman. David replied that they always kept themselves pure, even on ordinary missions, but, since this was an especially holy mission (another piece of deception!) they were taking especial care in this respect. So Ahimelech gave David the consecrated bread and he and his men ate it.

The whole point of Jesus quoting this story is that it involved the law being broken. He is mentioning this incident because it is an example of answer c) – a situation where special circumstances make it permissible to break the law – and he is drawing from the story the lesson that such situations do occur, in order to then argue that the situation of the disciples falls into the same category.

The story of David's visit to Ahimelech involves three infringements of God's law:

- First, David lied;
- Second, he ate the consecrated bread which the law said should be eaten only by priests;
- Third, to make it worse, he implicated his men by giving the bread to them.

But the circumstances justified it on a number of counts:

- he was running away from a murder threat. He was doing this to save himself and his men from being killed either by Saul or by starvation;
- he had the welfare of his men at heart.
- If he had not run from Saul, he would have had to fight him and, since Saul was God's anointed king, fighting him would draw David into greater sin. He didn't want to be cornered into becoming responsible for the death of God's anointed;
- furthermore, he was going to protect Saul from having blood on his hands if he killed David.

For all these reasons, there was justification for David to break the law. He was breaking it to achieve a higher good.

In Matthew's account of the same incident (Matthew 12), Jesus goes on to quote the example of the priests in the temple. They break God's law by working on the Sabbath when they offer sacrifices. They are working on the Sabbath but they are not guilty because they are carrying out God's instructions). The Sabbath law is cancelled out in this instance by a higher law. He then makes a stupendous claim:

"I tell you that something greater than the temple is here. If you had known what these words mean: 'I desire mercy, not sacrifice,' you would not have condemned the innocent. For the Son of Man is Lord of the Sabbath." (Matthew 12 v 7–8)

In these words Jesus is claiming that he has authority over the Sabbath – that he has the right to tell people whether they should keep the Sabbath or not and how they should observe it. He quotes some words of the prophet Hosea which are part of a Messianic prophecy.
They begin:

"Let us acknowledge the Lord,
Let us press on to acknowledge him.
As surely as the sun rises he will appear;
He will come to us like the winter rains,
Like the spring rains that water the earth."
(Hosea 6 v 3–4)

It is the coming Messiah who then says, in Hosea 6 v 6, "I desire mercy, not sacrifice and acknowledgement of God rather than burnt offerings." Jesus is claiming that he is the Lord about whom this passage speaks.

It is important to remember that the Sabbath law is one of the Ten Commandments. In his letter James says that if someone fails to keep one of the commandments he is guilty of breaking the whole law. For several decades now there has been a decline in Sabbath observance among Christians. Leaving aside the argument that crops up from time to time as to whether the proper day to observe the Sabbath is Sunday or Saturday, there has been a consistent erosion of Sunday observance in most Western countries. In the United States a visit to a fast food restaurant before or after church on Sunday is common practice. In the United Kingdom, attendance at church twice on a Sunday has dwindled to once for most Christians and the removal of Sunday trading restrictions has led to Sunday becoming indistinguishable from Saturday for most people. While most Christians still pay some lip service to the idea of keeping Sunday as a holy day, in practice most Christians regard the Sabbath Law as of less importance than other commandments, such as those against murder, adultery and theft. Yet the Bible puts them all on the same level. As James tells us, "He who breaks the law in one point breaks all of it." (James 2 v 10) If you don't observe the Sabbath, it is as bad in God's eyes as stealing or even murdering someone. So this is a big issue, not a matter of lesser importance.

This all drives me to the shocking conclusion that Jesus' response to the Pharisees is to say that there are times when the right thing to do is to set aside one of the Ten Commandments and that this is one such occasion. There can be situations where there is a matter of life and death and to keep the Law would result in a death. There are occasions when one Commandment apparently contradicts another which is more applicable. And, finally, there is the possibility that the Messiah himself, as giver of the Law, may countermand one commandment with another, contradicting the letter, but not the spirit of the Law. These situations do not involve breaking the law as a whole but do involve breaking one law in the process of fulfiling another.

The implications of this are far-reaching. Christians tend to regulate their behaviour and their condemnation of others according to law. The law that they apply includes not just the Old Testament moral law but the scriptures as a whole. To these they often add a whole set of behavioural norms accepted by their particular culture or church group. If no rules have been broken, we feel satisfied. On the other hand, we suppose, rules must be kept even if the result is to cause pain, hurt and injury to others. Jesus, however, was evidently willing to set aside the Law (the Sabbath Commandment) in order to help and heal others.

The Pharisees understood James's principle that breaking one commandment means breaking all of them. That's why they got so annoyed with Jesus and made such an issue of his approach to the Sabbath. If Jesus said there could be occasions when it was right to break the Sabbath Law, it implied that there might be occasions when it is right to break other commandments as well.

As the giver of the law, God is not bound by it. He has given the Law for a purpose and it is inconceivable that there could be occasions when God would want his law to be applied in a way that negated that purpose.

Even if the disciples walking through the cornfield were breaking the law by plucking ears of corn, Jesus was showing them mercy by allowing them to do so. As the Lord of the Sabbath he could do that. And the Pharisees were not showing mercy in their judgemental response.

Chapter eight

Test Cases

All three synoptic gospels follow the account of the disciples plucking corn on the Sabbath with another incident that also relates to the Sabbath. This incident is very important – so important that it marks the crucial turning point in the uneasy relationship between the Pharisees and Jesus. It eventually became, in human terms, the cause of his death.

The point at issue was whether it was lawful for Jesus to heal people on the Sabbath. Jesus was visiting a synagogue. In the congregation was a man who had a paralysed hand. Would Jesus heal him or not? It seems that the Pharisees had a "hunch" that he might do. If he did, in their view, he would be working on the Sabbath. It sounds very much as if they were waiting to catch him out.

It would, of course, have been perfectly possible for him to promise the man a healing if he returned the following day. The man had been ill for a long time and was not apparently in danger of death, so one day would have made little difference. That way, Jesus could have healed the man, kept the Sabbath law and retained the respect and support of the Pharisees. From the Pharisee point of view this was a good test. If Jesus was genuinely from God, he would wait until after the Sabbath to heal the man. They would find the combination of power to heal and respect for the law convincing.

But in the event, Jesus made an issue out of healing the man, even though it was the Sabbath. He was thus deliberately challenging the Pharisees' understanding of what was right.

Matthew provides us with some details that Mark and Luke leave out. According to him, it was the Pharisees who provoked the confrontation by asking Jesus, "Is it lawful to heal on the Sabbath?" Jesus must then have replied with the counter question that Mark records in his gospel,

> "Which is lawful on the Sabbath: to do good or to do evil, to save life or to kill?" (Mark 3 v 4)

It was an impossible question for the Pharisees to answer. Jesus had them in a corner. Either they had to give Jesus permission to heal on the Sabbath, or they had to say that the right thing was to prolong the man's suffering and thus be guilty of doing him harm. Since neither alternative was acceptable, they said nothing. There was a pregnant silence. Then, Matthew tells us, Jesus spoke again,

> "If any of you has a sheep and it falls into a pit on he Sabbath, will you not take hold of it and lift it out? How much more valuable is a person than a sheep! Therefore it is lawful to do good on the Sabbath." (Matthew 12 v 11–12)

What followed was a dramatic moment. This was the turning point. Mark says that Jesus "Looked round at them in anger, deeply distressed at their stubborn hearts." Then he told the man to stretch out his hand. The man's hand was completely restored.

All three synoptic gospel writers agree that immediately, in response to this incident, the Pharisees began to plot together to have Jesus killed. As they saw it, Jesus was dangerous. He was advocating that people should disregard God's law. It has been suggested that the Pharisees plotted to kill Jesus from a motive of jealousy because he was attracting a greater following than they were. That credits the Pharisees with extremely selfish and hypocritical motives. I think we can give them more credence than that. I believe they were genuinely anxious to promote righteousness and that their opposition came about, not from selfish jealousy but from their outrage at a supposed Messiah who, as they saw it, had no respect for God's law and was encouraging others to share that lack of respect.

This was the start of the movement of opposition to Jesus. Bearing in mind the numerical strength of the Pharisees and their connections in high places, it is possible to say, in causal terms, this is why Jesus was crucified. This is where the process began that led to his death.

John records a further occasion when Jesus clashed with the Pharisees over the same issue, later in his ministry. A man was brought to the Pharisees who had been blind from birth until Jesus told him, on the Sabbath, to go and wash his eyes in the pool of Siloam. The man had followed Jesus' instructions and, ever since, he had been able to see. The Pharisees were eager to quench the understandable enthusiasm that the man and his parents had developed for Jesus. John records:

> "Some of the Pharisees said, 'This man is not from God, for he does not keep the Sabbath.'" (John 9 v 16)

They were judging by very limited criteria. They could have asked, "Does this man fulfil the prophecies about the Messiah?" This does not seem to have come into consideration for them. They could have asked, "Does he reflect Gods character?" But they didn't. Their eyes were fixed solely on the question of obedience to the law. They do not appear for one moment to have considered, "Could we be wrong in our understanding of the law?"

We can all too easily follow in their footsteps today, judging people by the wrong criteria. It is all too easy to set up our own invalid criteria and apply them to one another, with potentially disastrous results:

> "This man cannot be from God because he speaks in tongues (or doesn't, as the case may be)."
>
> "This woman cannot be from God; look at the way she dresses..."

> "That preacher can't have the anointing of the Holy Spirit; he uses the wrong Bible translation."
>
> "That church cannot be experiencing God's best because it belongs to the wrong denomination (or the wrong apostolic stream)".

The Sabbath law seems to have been the start of the conflict but the issue was to do with the law of God as a whole. Soon other issues came into question. One such issue was the question of divorce. This was a live issue at the time. Two noted rabbis had disagreed over the issue:

> **Rabbi Hillel** argued that a man could divorce his wife if he was displeased with her for any reason.
>
> **Rabbi Shammai** argued that a man could only divorce his wife if she had committed adultery.

Which view would Jesus support? The Pharisees brought the question to him. Jesus' response, recorded in Matthew 19, was to reiterate the basic principle of lifelong, monogamous marriage, referring them back to the creation of Adam and Eve. However, the Pharisees pressed Jesus:

> "Why then ... did Moses *command* that a man give his wife a certificate of divorce and send her away?" (Matthew 19 v 7)

The word "command" is significant; as he replied, Jesus pointedly altered the word the Pharisees had used:

> "Moses *permitted* you to divorce your wives because your hearts were hard." (Matthew 19 v 8)

The emphasis is mine here but I suspect that Jesus put an emphasis on the word "permitted" as he spoke it. In their legalistic mindset, the Pharisees had read the relevant passage in the book of Deuteronomy as a command that in certain situations they should divorce their wives because that was the righteous thing to do. In so doing, the husband expressed his disapproval of the wife's wrongdoing and disassociated himself from it. The Pharisees could only understand the law in restrictive terms. The law was there to tell tem what they couldn't do. With the change of word from "command" to "permit", Jesus turned this on its head. The law was there, not to restrict them, but to safeguard their freedom. God intended it to clarify for us what we *can* do. It was positive, not negative. There were even situations, like this one, where God's Law said, effectively, "You may do this – but you don't have to." God had given the law about divorce to regulate something that was generally against his will. He gave it to protect women and children who might otherwise be put out on the streets without means of support, or separated from one another by a man's whim to divorce his wife. This permissive law allowed men to divorce their wives but stipulated that they had to provide a legal document to say so. It was an expression of mercy and compassion rather than condemnation and judgement.

The idea of a permissive law was one which the Pharisees found it hard to grasp. It turned all their ideas about God and the law upside-down. From their point of view it seemed that Jesus was saying that the law didn't matter. You could disregard the Sabbath, divorce your wife (or husband) at whim – even worse, you could forgive them if they committed adultery, thus condoning their sin.

Of course, this was a misrepresentation of Jesus' position. Jesus did not advocate doing away with the law. As we have seen in the Sermon on the Mount, he honoured the law and said he was advocating a higher standard of obedience that that of the Pharisees. He urged people not to ignore what the Pharisees taught:

> "The teachers of the law and the Pharisees sit in Moses' seat. So you must be careful to do everything they tell you."
>
> (Matthew 23 v 2)

The difference was that Jesus saw the law as a means to an end while the Pharisees saw it as an end in itself. Jesus did not see the law as something given by a disapproving God solely as a basis for punishing sinners (although he did clearly warn of a judgement to come). For him, the law was an expression of the love of God, given to regulate behaviour so that relationships were preserved and people were protected from harm. God's intention was for us to keep the law first and foremost as an expression of love and worship towards him, and secondly as a way of honouring other people as his creatures. The law was an expression of God's heart and was to be interpreted accordingly. It was not the letter of the law that was important but the heart of God to which it gave expression.

For the Pharisees, the law was detached from any sense of relationship with God. Following the letter of the law did not require them to interact personally with God in any way. God had spoken and given them the law which was final and complete. They did not expect to hear anything more from God. They needed nothing else. As a result they didn't look to God with expectancy in an ongoing relationship.

In this they were not unlike some Christians today who think that, because God has revealed himself through the Bible, he has nothing more to say. They reject the idea that God might continue to speak to them through gifts of the Spirit and see any openness to prophetic gifts as undermining the authority of the Bible. The Pharisees were closed off in the same way to hearing anything new from God. They had traded a dynamic relationship with a living God for a dead tradition. Jesus applied some words from Isaiah to describe their lack of relationship with God:

> "These people honour me with their lips,
> But their hearts are far from me.
> They worship me in vain;
> Their teachings are but rules taught by men."
>
> (Matthew 15 v 8 and 9)

In contrast, Jesus taught his disciples to keep the law in the context of a living relationship with God.

The Pharisees could not understand Jesus' approach to the law. It shocked and angered them, so much so that they began to see Jesus as a threat to the spiritual welfare of the crowds that flocked to hear him and to the very structure of their society. They couldn't grasp the truth, on which Jesus was operating, that the Law was a means to an end and the end was more important than the means. In a sense the Law was their security and Jesus threatened it.

As the account of Jesus' ministry in the gospels unfolds, the Pharisees begin to constantly probe Jesus by bringing test questions to see how he would deal with them. I get the impression that they were trying to gather evidence which would enable them to convict and condemn him and yet, at the same time, were trying to fathom out where Jesus was coming from, how he could claim to be a messenger from God and yet, apparently, condone breaking the law.

They were completely shocked by things Jesus was saying and doing. In fact, it is possible to see in the Pharisees' reactions all the characteristics of the kind of denial that people go through in times of shock or grief, after a trauma or a bereavement. Jesus has shaken the foundations of their security. They think he is proposing that the Law of God can be set aside. They think it, but it is so shocking that they can't bring themselves to believe that it could be true. Consequently, they keep returning to the issue, testing and testing again, hoping to hear Jesus explain that he didn't really mean what they thought he had said. But, time and time again, they fail to be satisfied by Jesus' replies.

Time after time, they fail to hear what they want to hear. In the end, rather than really listening to Jesus and risking having to face up to the unacceptable, they decide to blot Jesus out in a classic denial reaction.

Several incidents all form part of this pattern: the encounter with the woman caught in adultery, arguments about paying temple taxes and taxes to Caesar – all of these formed part of the testing process as the Pharisees tried to either prove themselves mistaken about Jesus, or to prove Jesus worthy of death.

However, it wasn't a one-sided antagonism. It wasn't simply that the Pharisees opposed Jesus as a result of misunderstanding his teaching. He did understand them, only too well, and he was active and vocal in his opposition to them.

Matthew records some key developments in the conflict between Jesus and the Pharisees in the twelfth chapter of his gospel; our next chapter carefully analyses this account.

Chapter nine

The Conflict

The crowd around Jesus parted as a little group of people passed through. They were leading by the hand a man who had a pitiable level of disability – he was both blind and dumb. The combination of these disabilities in itself would have been bad enough but blindness and inability to speak were only the tip of an iceberg. Although the symptoms were physical, this was not a medical problem. A deeper cause lay behind the presenting symptoms. Dark powers had been at work in this man's life. It may have been the result of his own folly and rebellion in getting involved in the forbidden dark side of the spiritual realm. Alternatively, he might have been under some kind of curse.

Whatever the cause, Jesus went straight to the heart of the situation and addressed the demon which was causing the symptoms. The effect on the man was electrifying. He recovered his sight and began to talk excitedly, the pent up frustration of the silent years gushing out in a sudden flood of communication. The crowd went wild with excitement. The enthusiasm of the crowd grew as people talked about what they had seen. Some began to speculate, "Could this be the Son of David – the Messiah who has been promised? Is this it? Is the kingdom of God about to begin?

A small group of Pharisees stood among the crowd, not joining in the hubbub of excitement but watching with stern and troubled faces. The

Pharisees had only recently decided that Jesus was a moral danger to the people and so his activity would have to be stopped. But now the swell of interest was becoming a flood tide. The Pharisees began to consider how they could dampen people's enthusiasm and warn them off Jesus. As they saw it, Jesus was not keeping the law and therefore did not merit God's approval, so therefore, whatever spiritual power or authority he had must have come from the only other possible source – Satan. They would tell the people,

> "It is only by Beelzebub, the prince of demons, that this fellow drives out demons." (Matthew 12 v 24).

But before ever they had a chance to express the thought, Jesus was already contradicting them with the uncanny habit he had of answering the thoughts in people's minds before they opened their mouths to express them. His logic was just as sharp:

> "If Satan drives out Satan, he is divided against himself. How then can his kingdom stand? And if I drive out demons by Beelzebub, by whom do your people drive them out? So then, they will be your judges. But if I drive out demons by the Spirit of God, then the kingdom of God has come upon you." (Matthew 12 v 26–28)

Then suddenly Jesus rounded on the group of Pharisees. With a sharpness of tongue that was new and unexpected, he looked at them and almost spat out the words:

> "You viper's brood, how can you who are evil say anything good? For out of the overflow of the heart the mouth speaks..."
> (Matthew 12 v 34)

Satan, as everyone knew, had appeared to Eve as a snake and Jesus was now calling them a snake's brood. Jesus was branding them as the offspring of Satan rather than children of Eve. He was, in effect, saying, "It isn't I who am in league with Satan; you Pharisees are like a clutch of eggs hatched out by the Devil himself – reproductions of the enemy of God, ready to spread your poison to turn people against the Almighty. Far from being representatives of God's law, you are actually opposing what God is doing and, worse still, attributing acts of God to Satan."

Jesus had humiliated the Pharisees over the Sabbath question. Now it was "round two" to Jesus as well, as he "wiped the floor" with them once more, taking them by surprise with the vehemence of his attack.

The Pharisees couldn't ignore it. To walk away would have been to lose face in front of the crowd. They responded, though their next move involved a change of tack which is not easy to fathom. Continuing to follow this interaction through Matthew chapter 12, we find that Matthew records:

> "Then some of the Pharisees and teachers of the law said to him, 'Teacher, we want to see a sign from you.'"
>
> (Matthew 12 v 38)

What kind of sign were they looking for? Only a few moments earlier they had seen Jesus eject a demon from a man who had been blind and dumb. The man must at that moment still have been talking enthusiastically before their eyes about the things he could now see, to which he had previously been blind, and telling people all the things he'd previously wanted to say but been unable to articulate. This would have been sign enough for most people but it obviously wasn't enough for the Pharisees! Casting out a demon and causing a blind and dumb man to both see and hear wasn't enough. They were in touch with other miracle workers and exorcists who could claim things just as amazing and in any case they could find ways to explain it away. What they were asking for was something on a new level entirely – something they couldn't argue with. They were asking for something of the order of an angelic appearance or on a level with Elijah calling down fire from heaven or Moses dividing the Red Sea.

The problem is, when a sceptic asks for a miraculous sign, you know you are onto a loser. A confirmed unbeliever will always find a way to excuse their unbelief. Not surprisingly, Jesus didn't immediately oblige them.

> 'A wicked and adulterous generation asks for a sign, but no sign will be given it, except the sign of Jonah. For as Jonah was three days and nights in the belly of a huge fish, so the son of man will be three days and three nights in the heart of the earth."
>
> (Matthew 12 v 39–40)

Traditionally, people have viewed these words as a prediction of Jesus' death and resurrection. In a sense it is, but experts in Bible interpretation believe there is a possibility that the second sentence, was not actually spoken by Jesus – the one beginning "...for as Jonah was three days and nights in the belly of a huge fish..." The theory is that it was added, after the event, either by Matthew himself as he wrote the gospel, or perhaps by a scribe who added it as an explanatory note in the margin which then got taken into the main text. This view gains some small support from the fact that, when Luke refers to the same saying in his gospel (Luke 11 v 30), he omits the second part. If we assume that this theory is true and leave out the "explanatory note", what are we left with?

Jonah refused to trust God and, in disobedience, headed off in the opposite direction. As a result, he came under God's discipline. When the storm came, perhaps he began to think, "Maybe I should have obeyed and trusted God?" "As he hit the water, the thought grew stronger still. And, when he found himself inside the fish, he knew.

"And you'll know too" is what Jesus is saying to the Pharisees, "When God's judgment hits you." There was an obvious link with the resurrection but that may not have been the main thrust of what Jesus was saying. The "sign of Jonah" meant the judgment of God – the moment of hitting the water when your mind registers, "I was wrong! I couldn't get away with it, after all!"

The Pharisees were closed off to God doing anything new. There are Christians today who will refuse to accept that God can speak or act miraculously and, even when faced with a miracle, will find some argument to explain it away. They can be compared to the Pharisees of Jesus' day. Their religion is just a matter of holding to the "right" doctrines and doing the right things. They speak of faith but practise unbelief. Unless they repent and begin to trust, they too will face the storm of God's discipline.

So it was "round three to Jesus" as well. The Pharisees must have been starting to feel a little sore! We've begun to understand why the Pharisees were opposing Jesus – but why was Jesus so implacable and forceful in his opposition to them?

It wasn't personal. As we shall see later on, Jesus could be loving and patient when dealing with a Pharisee as an individual. It was what they represented that Jesus opposed. They represented the antithesis of the kingdom of God that he had come to bring. Jesus came to put God back in charge. The kingdom of God is the realm where God acts. To be in the kingdom means both experiencing God's power and acknowledging his authority. The kingdom of God is about mercy being offered to sinners and the help of the Holy Spirit being made available to people who can do nothing to save or help themselves.

On the surface, the Pharisees seemed to be seeking God's kingdom because they emphasised obedience to God's laws. But, in fact, theirs was a kingdom of human endeavour. The credit for them keeping the law went to them, not God. It was self-effort pure and simple. Yet Jesus had not come to tell people to pull themselves up by their own bootstraps. He had come to tell them that, when they had "blown it", when there were sinful thoughts and reactions that they struggled with but couldn't get the better of, then the mercy and power of God was there to provide forgiveness and the ability to change. He came to die as a sacrifice so that sinners could be justly forgiven. If you can keep the law in your own strength, you don't need a saviour. There was a risk that, by following the Pharisees' lead and ignoring Jesus, people would miss out on eternal salvation. It was vital for Jesus to make it plain that there was clear water between him and the Pharisees. Considering what was at stake, it is no wonder that he became so animated and forceful as he laboured to make plain the differences between the Pharisees and himself.

After the incident with the blind and dumb man, the Pharisees seem to have withdrawn for a while. Perhaps they reasoned that, as long as the

Jesus movement stayed in Galilee, they could ignore it. Maybe the local Pharisees in Galilee realised they were no match for Jesus. However, when Jesus moved south to Jerusalem, the conflict started to heat up again. News of Jesus' activities and beliefs must have spread along the Pharisee grapevine, so that, when he arrived, the "big guns" in the capital were ready. Even so, it must have been quite unnerving for them when Jesus rode into Jerusalem on a donkey, surrounded by a jubilant crowd of supporters. The significance of the donkey would not have been lost on the Bible-reading Pharisaical scribes. They would have recognised it as a bid for Messiahship. The discussion among the Pharisees about how to get rid of Jesus became more urgent.

Within their terms of reference, they were faced with a major problem. They had to act within the law which, of course, banned them from killing him, unless he could be proved guilty of a capital offence. The Pharisee mind is capable of unbelievable contortions when the demands of the law contradict what a Pharisee desires or feels to be right. They wanted Jesus dead. They were plotting to bring his death about. But they couldn't just hire a hit man to take him out; the law clearly said, "You shall not kill." Killing was only allowed in the Old Testament law as a punishment for serious crimes such as murder or adultery. The law would allow them to have Jesus killed – but only if he had done something that merited a capital punishment.

There was no chance of them pinning a charge of murder or adultery on Jesus but the two charges that might stick were those of blasphemy or treachery. If they could prove that Jesus had uttered blasphemy, they could kill him according to Jewish law. If he said something against Caesar, they could report it to the Roman Governor and he would do the rest.

One of the Pharisees thought of a simple question which was guaranteed to trap Jesus. However Jesus answered it, he would be forced to shoot himself in the foot. So a group of Pharisees came to ask him the question,

> "Is it right to pay the poll tax to Caesar or not?" (Mark 12 v 14)

The taxes paid to the Romans were notoriously unpopular. In the event that Jesus said people should pay taxes to Rome, they could spread the word that he was disloyal, unJewish, a traitor to his country and people. They could turn the crowds against him and reduce his support. With a bit of luck one of the fiercely nationalistic zealots would slit his throat on a dark night, thus doing the Pharisees' job for them. On the other hand, if Jesus said that it *wasn't* necessary to pay taxes to Caesar, then they could hand him over to the Romans for immediate execution.

The way Jesus sidestepped this challenge is among the most famous incidents in the Bible. Jesus asked to see a Roman coin, a denarius. "Whose image is this?" he asked. "Caesar's", they replied. "Give to Caesar what is Caesar's and to God what is God's," said Jesus.

It was a masterful reply.

There was a rival group among the Jewish leadership, not as strong in numbers as the Pharisees but still commanding wealth and influence. The Sadducees rejected the Pharisees' rigid legalism and also what they saw as a gullible fascination on the Pharisees' part with the supernatural – angels, demons, resurrection and life beyond the grave. They poured scorn on all of these. There was a rivalry between the two groups and it is tempting to imagine that, having seen Jesus humiliate the Pharisees, the Sadducees thought they would try to get one over their rivals by getting the better of Jesus themselves.

Mark tells us that, on the same day as the Pharisees brought the question about paying taxes to Caesar, the Sadducees also came to Jesus with a challenging question. They proposed a situation where a woman had had seven husbands, been widowed seven times and then died herself. "In the resurrection," they asked, "whose wife would she be?"

At least one Pharisee must have been standing by and spread the word to his friends about the way Jesus answered the Sadducees. As he did so they must have had a strange mixture of emotions because Jesus had given the Sadducees an answer the Pharisees would have been proud of:

> "Are you not in error because you do not know the Scriptures or the Power of God? When the dead rise, they will neither marry nor be given in marriage; they will be like the angels in heaven. Now about the dead rising – have you not read in the Book of Moses, in the account of the burning bush, how God said to him 'I am the God of Abraham, the God of Isaac and the God of Jacob'? He is not the God of the dead but of the living. You are badly mistaken" (Mark 12 v 25¬27)

You can imagine the kind of report any Pharisee would have made to his friends, "Jesus really sorted out those Sadducees – you should have seen their faces! His answer was brilliant …"

Jesus had exposed two fundamental errors in the Sadducees' position – they disregarded the Scriptures and ignored the power of God. At the same time he had given scriptural proof of the resurrection, pointing out that God didn't say, "I *was* the God of Abraham, Isaac and Jacob", but "I *am*…" Therefore they still exist.

"Aha! Got you Sadducees!" It was just the kind of hair-splitting Bible interpretation that the Pharisees loved.

Perhaps because of the way Jesus had responded to the Sadducees, his next public encounter with the Pharisees had a more friendly feel to it. "Teacher," one of them asked him, "which is the greatest commandment in the Law?" It could have been a trap ("However he answers we can contradict him") but it sounds more like a genuine enquiry. The Pharisee asking the question is described as "an expert in the Law". This was a man who loved the Old Testament and recognised in Jesus a fellow enthusiast. Like one computer geek talking to another or two bird-watchers in a wildlife sanctuary, this Pharisee wanted to talk shop with someone who could match his interest. We don't know if this expert had already noticed that all the commandments can be fitted under one or other of two headings, "Love the Lord your God," or "Love your neighbour." In any case, Jesus showed him and he was impressed.

Then Jesus asked him a question. Tongue in cheek, Jesus gently nudged the Pharisee and his accompanying friends into a corner, using this cosy chat between experts to present them with a thorny problem of interpretation that forced the expert in the Law into a *cul de sac*. For any Sadducees listening in, Jesus' question gave them problems too, so they had no reason to gloat:

> "'What do you think about the Messiah? Whose son is he?'
> 'The Son of David,' they replied.
> He said to them, 'How is it then that David, speaking by the Spirit, calls him "Lord"? For he says,
> 'The Lord said to my Lord:
> "Sit at my right hand until I put your enemies under your feet."'
> If David calls him, 'Lord', how can he be his son?"
>
> (Matthew 22 v 41–45)

One of the commandments said, "Honour your father and your mother." This was part of a wider system which the Jews fully recognised and accepted, that those who had precedence and authority were to be honoured. The promised Messiah would be a king in David's line. Therefore they expected that the Messiah, as David's descendant, would give honour to David, his ancestor. However, the quotation Jesus cited from Psalm 110 has David honouring the Messiah.

Looking back with hindsight through centuries of Christian thought and teaching, we know the answer to the question Jesus asked them. The Messiah may be a physical descendant of David but he is also the Son of God – God made manifest in the flesh. Spiritually, the Son of God has been in existence since before the foundation of the world and David owed his very existence, along with all of creation, to the One who is the Creative Word of God.

The Spirit of God, speaking through David, knew this and put these words into his mind to indicate that the Messiah was on a higher level, meriting honour from David. But, of course, the Pharisees didn't know that. Jesus had posed them a question to which they didn't know the answer. As the expert exponents of the Law of God, they were supposed to know all the answers but they couldn't answer this question. Jesus was very gently, and very charmingly, humiliating them in front of the watching crowd.

At the same time, Jesus was opening their minds to the awesome thought that the coming Messiah was going to be bigger than they imagined and, if Jesus knew this, maybe he was the One. He was hinting very strongly that he might be greater than David, than Moses, even than Abraham – without actually saying it. They didn't like what he was suggesting but they couldn't refute it and, since he had only hinted at it, they couldn't condemn him for it.

Meanwhile, for the Sadducees who were listening in, Jesus' question raised the awkward possibility of someone existing before David but coming after him and, in the intervening time, living on in some other existence which, as Sadducees, they weren't allowed to believe in.

No wonder that Matthew comments,

> "From that day on, no one dared to ask him any more questions."
> (Matthew 22 v 46)

Chapter ten

The Seven Woes

The Pharisees may have been left speechless at the end of this last encounter with Jesus, but Jesus still had plenty to say. In the account in Matthew's gospel Jesus immediately began to talk about the Pharisees to the crowd.

He starts on a positive note:

> "The Pharisees sit in Moses' seat. They devote themselves to teaching the law that God gave to us through Moses. You must be careful to do everything they do...

But then comes the "but…". He quickly moves into a whole chapter of criticism of the Pharisees, beginning,

> "... but do not do what they do, for they do not practise what they preach. They tie up heavy, cumbersome loads and put them on other people'sshoulders, but they themselves are not willing to lift a finger to move them." (Matthew 23 v 2–4)

At some length, Jesus took them apart, exposing their motives of performance orientation and seeking approval for themselves and making fun of their love of titles of honour and dressing up to be noticed.

The way I like to imagine it, the group of Pharisees had not yet left the scene at the point when Jesus said these words. I suspect they had moved away from Jesus but had stopped just within sight and earshot – across the street and a little way down it, perhaps, or on the other side of one of the courtyards in the temple. I picture them standing in a little huddle, still discussing David and the Messiah, and trying to think of a way to turn the tables on the way Jesus has just humiliated them in public debate. While they are talking together, Jesus raises his voice and calls to them, speaking loudly enough for them to hear:

> "Woe to you, teachers of the law and Pharisees, you hypocrites!"

"Woe to you" is an old English expression that meant "Watch it" or "You've got it coming to you!"

Jesus then launched into a series of seven statements, each of which condemned the Pharisees for a different aspect of their behaviour. Jesus was not venting his own anger here – that would have been sin. He was expressing God's anger. The pattern of seven statements is significant because in the Bible the number seven is always a symbol of completeness. This symbolism springs from the fact that God rested on the seventh day after completing the creation. So condemning the Pharisees seven times had a kind of ritual effect; it indicated that Jesus was officially pronouncing God's absolute condemnation of them.

I find the seven statements interesting, and not a little disturbing, because they bear a close relationship to trends that I observe among many present day Christians and, more to the point, in myself. These tendencies indicate that the Pharisee spirit is, unfortunately, alive and active in the church today. Each of Jesus' statements has its parallel in modern day church life, particularly in the Evangelical wing of the Christian community.

Let me make it clear that I am criticising from inside, not from outside. I am an Evangelical myself. I am a member of a church that belongs to the Evangelical Alliance. I believe the Bible is inspired by God and is the only authority for our faith and practise. I believe God meets us through its pages. I believe in substitutionary atonement and I look back with gratitude to the whole Evangelical tradition from Luther and Calvin through Whitfield, Wesley and Wilberforce all the way down to Wimber and Willow Creek. Nevertheless, I have come to believe that we Evangelicals are dangerously close in spirit to the Pharisees of Jesus' time. I am not saying that Evangelicalism is a form of Pharisaism, because the essence of Evangelicalism is grace and grace and legalism are incompatible. What I am saying is that because of our reverence for Scripture, Evangelicals are more prone to Pharisaism than the followers of other brands of Christianity and that too often we allow ourselves to slip into Pharisee ways of thinking and acting. If you take grace away from Evangelicalism, Pharisaism is all you have left, and there are too many Evangelicals who have either lost sight of the grace of God, or who have never properly grasped it. Among such Evangelicals, the hallmarks of the Pharisee spirit are still to be found.

Let me be kinder, and identify myself with this because, like so many others, I also lose sight of God's grace too easily and find myself time and time again becoming a crabby Pharisee, condemning others, looking for approval, complaining if I don't get it, and adjusting God's law by reinterpreting Scripture so I stay on the right side of it. And, like the Pharisees, I am a hypocrite. My outward behaviour falls disastrously short of the standard I proclaim to be right. My words and my actions and my secret thought life do not match up.

Having said all that, Pharisaism is by no means restricted to the Evangelical wing of the church. You can't be a real Pharisee without an Evangelical view of the Bible but you will find plenty of Catholics and Liberals who show pronounced Pharisee tendencies without it. Their law-book may not be the Bible. It may be the accumulated dogmatism of left-wing theologians, or the accepted teaching of the Catholic wing of the Church..."teachings of men", which they treat with the same reverence as the Pharisees showed towards their accumulated body of accepted interpretations of the law of Moses.

However uncomfortable it may be, we need to pay attention to these "Woe to you" statements if we are going to be faithful to Jesus in our generation. Let's examine them one by one.

First Woe – I don't believe it so I won't let you believe it either

> "Woe to you, teachers of the law and Pharisees, you hypocrites! You shut the kingdom of heaven in people's faces. You yourselves do not enter, nor will you let those enter who are trying to."
> (Matthew 23 v 13)

That's the first of Jesus' seven broadsides. To understand it you first need to grasp what Jesus means by "The kingdom of heaven". As we have already observed, the kingdom of heaven is God's government – God's rule. And the "kingdom of God" is the same thing. Jews often used the word "heaven" as a substitute for "God", because they reasoned that God is too holy to be mentioned. The word "kingdom" is not a good translation of the Greek word *basileia*. "Kingdom" suggests geographic territory but the kingdom of God doesn't exist on a map, or a chart of the universe. The word *basileia* means "kingly rule". It refers to the decisions a king makes and the effectiveness with which he carries them out. A better translation of "the kingdom of God" would thus be "the sphere of God's government".

Whole books have been written on the subject, but the New Testament teaching about the kingdom of God can be summarised as follows:

God sent Jesus, his Son, to rule – first over the nation of Judah, but then over the whole earth. Mankind rejected Jesus' kingship, but God used that rejection to his own purpose and our good. One of the main ingredients of God's government is the offer of mercy and pardon for sinners. God has set a day when he will judge everyone who has ever lived on this earth and will correct any injustices which have taken place in human history. He will bring to account those who have got away with sin. He will hear the cases of those who have been abused and victimised. He will vindicate those who have been treated unjustly and give appropriate punishment to all those who have acted from selfish motives and disregarded God's commands (this unfortunately means everyone, because everyone has sinned). God has committed the responsibility for that judgement to his Son, Jesus, the King himself. In preparation for that day the King, who is going to judge us himself, offered to God on behalf of his subjects the perfectly obedient life we have all failed to live, crowning that achievement by obediently going to the cross to die, in our place, taking the punishment for our sin on himself. God now offers us forgiveness, but in order to receive that forgiveness we must repent (change the way we think) put our trust in him and become his servants and subjects.

Those who do become his subjects in that way are enlisted in the task of extending his kingdom by calling others to become his subjects too. To assist them in the task, he makes the miraculous power of the Holy Spirit available to them, together with the miraculous gifts of the Holy Spirit. He also calls them to relate together in a new way, basing their treatment of each other on the love and grace he has shown to them. Finally, He promises that, by a certain time known only to God Himself, a representative number of people from each linguistic, ethnic, political and social group will voluntarily become his subjects and, at that point, Jesus will return for the day of judgement. After the judgement, those whom he recognises as his will live with him forever in a new universe where the barrier between earth and heaven no longer exists.

This message of the kingdom is all about grace. The Kingdom is not something we bring about, it is something God does. It is not an empire created by human effort, it consists of things that God gives. The benefits of the kingdom are not a reward for good behaviour. The blessings of the kingdom – forgiveness, the power and gifts of the Holy Spirit, and the life to come – are all an expression of God's grace and mercy to people who don't deserve to be part of it. We can't make the kingdom happen, we can only pray for it to come and try to co-operate with it when it does. In essence, the Kingdom has already begun. God has begun to act, even though he still has a lot more to do. King Jesus has taken his throne. He has been crowned. He is already establishing his kingdom and, although we cannot yet experience it in its fullness, we can live in its power and under its authority right where we are – unless you are a Pharisee, that is, because Pharisaism and the kingdom of God are incompatible.

Pharisees expect to earn forgiveness by doing penance, or preferably to keep their noses clean so they don't need mercy in the first place. They don't need the Holy Spirit, because they expect to be good and to serve God in their own strength. Because of what they believe, they do not come to a place where they can begin to experience the amazing reality of the kingdom of God.

Pharisees are free to make that choice. But what Jesus objected to was that, by pressing their belief in self-effort on others, the Pharisees were preventing those people from experiencing the kingdom. Rather than telling people how much they need God's mercy and how they can receive it, they were telling people how bad they were and how they really should try harder to be good. That's why Jesus said, "You shut the kingdom of heaven in men's faces."

More than anything else, this was the main quarrel that Jesus had with the Pharisees. This is why he showed them so little mercy and even showed signs of being angry with them. He had come to establish the kingdom of God and to encourage people to live in it. But the Pharisees, with their teaching about the law, effectively closed the door to the kingdom and stood in front of it, pointing people in another direction.

Two thousand years on, there are people within the Christian Church today who, like the Pharisees, hedge the faith around with rules and regulations and traditions of men, to such a degree that they make it difficult for others to experience the grace of God. There are those who deny those sovereign actions of God that the Bible calls the gifts of the Holy Spirit. They would have us believe they ceased with the apostles. They say that we don't need living contact with God through prayer and prophecy, because we have the Bible. Whether they are denying others the assurance of forgiveness or trying to stop them from experiencing the grace-gifts which come through the Holy Spirit, they are locking the door to the kingdom of God, refusing to go in themselves, and refusing to let anyone else in either.

Second Woe – Evangelistic zeal without concern for righteousness

One of the distinguishing features of Evangelical Christianity is its evangelistic zeal. For many Evangelicals, "thou shalt witness" is an eleventh commandment added to the original ten. I grew up among Evangelical Christians and over the years I have heard preacher after preacher castigate their hearers for their reluctance to speak openly about their faith. Missionary zeal is one of the hallmarks of Evangelical Christianity. Evangelicalism has spawned a host of para-church agencies and missions geared to fulfiling the Great Commission by making disciples from all nations. Go to the deserts of North Africa, the depths of the Amazon rain forest, the remotest Siberian waste or the most isolated island in the South Pacific, and you will find there an Evangelical Christian who has travelled from some other part of the world to preach the gospel and persuade people to repent and believe in Jesus.

> "You travel over land and sea to win a single convert."

Jesus could easily have been talking to Evangelicals here.

Please note that I am not condemning evangelism and missionary enterprise, nor was Jesus. It is the next part which contains the condemnation:

> "But when you succeed, you make him twice as much a child of hell as you are." (Matthew 23 v 15)

Like modern day Evangelicals, the Pharisees were eager to make converts. They wanted Gentiles to believe in God and to become Jews, and they went to great lengths to achieve this aim. However, what they did with the converts afterwards, was inadequate. Having discovered a loving, gracious God, the converts were quickly bound up with rules and regulations and infected with the self-glorifying poison of Pharisee religion.

I sometimes feel uncomfortable with the way we teach new Christians in Evangelical churches. We thrill them with the gospel of grace and forgiveness. We tell them there is absolutely nothing they can do to save themselves, and that all their righteous deeds are like filthy rags in God s sight. Then, as soon as we get a commitment out of them, we hand them a new list of commandments: read your Bible every day, pray twice a day, go to church twice on Sunday, attend a homegroup, go to the prayer meeting, tell everyone at work you have become a Christian, give a tenth of your income to God's work, witness to your neighbours, get involved with social issues, and so on.

Other sections of the church are little better. The rules are just different. If you are a Liberal you just have a different set of laws, which might include: "Thou shalt oppose racism, sexism and inadequate social security benefits, instead of "Thou shalt oppose pornography, abortion and Sunday Trading." Instead of turning converts to Christ and making them like him, we turn converts to our idea of Christianity and make them conform to the norms of our denomination or group, just as the Pharisees did. At best, converts are left to their own devices, like babies abandoned at birth. At worst they become infected with all the legalism of their fellow Christians. And, just as the original Pharisees focused their attention on the minutiae of the law and became blind to greater issues of social justice, so many Christians today, in their eagerness to win converts, neglect what Jesus called the "weightier matters of the law" and encourage their converts to do the same.

Third Woe – Legalism with loopholes

One of the consequences of a Pharisee-like preoccupation with the letter of the law is that, having drawn, as it were, a line in the sand to show the point where the law is broken, we are tempted to see how close we can get to the line without, technically, crossing it. Rather than truly hating wrongdoing, Pharisees wish they could break the law but they stay on the right side of it out of other motives, such as fear of punishment or desire for acceptance and praise.

Instead of aiming for the best that the spirit of the law inspires us to, we settle for the minimum that the letter of the law requires. We step up to the supposed line and stand with our toes on it, telling ourselves, "I haven't crossed the line!" We stand there, savouring the temptation and eventually give in, promising, "I've only stepped over for a moment and I'm going to step back again very soon!" We end up stepping backwards and forwards over the line, convincing ourselves that we are on the right side more often than we are on the wrong side and that eventually, we will stay on the right side for good. We look for loopholes that we can exploit to adjust the law to suit ourselves because we have no way of coping with a situation where we fail to keep our own standards.

It's a pattern that is very common:

> "Technically, I'm only borrowing it for a little while. I intend to return it." Says the thief.
>
> "It's partly true, I'm just not telling the whole story", says the liar.
>
> "It's not adultery. We haven't, technically, had sex," says the married man or the married woman drifting into a secret romantic friendship.

And when a Pharisaical Christian catches someone else in sin, their response is likely to be,

> "I know Jesus says I should forgive you and I will – but not until you've been adequately punished and proved that your repentance is real."

Respect for scriptural authority degenerates into a quest for a biblical loophole, some way of interpreting the Bible that will enable us to justify our dishonesty, our immorality or our resentful hardness of heart.

The Pharisees made full use of loopholes they found in the law as Jesus pointed out;

> "Woe to you, blind guides! You say, 'If anyone swears by the temple, it means nothing: but if anyone swears by the gold of the temple, he is bound by his oath.'" (Matthew 23 v 16)

The reason for distinguishing between different oaths in this way was to provide a way to be excused from keeping promises they had made. They were sacrificing the principle of covenant-keeping under the guise of a strict adherence to the letter of the law.

Fourth Woe – Tithing without generosity

Different cultures have different senses of humour. There is a lot of humour in Jesus' sayings, which we often miss, because we don't understand first century Jewish humour, which Jesus used to good effect. It relied a lot on exaggeration. The crowd would have laughed at his picture of the Pharisees taking their measuring sticks to separate off every tenth centimetre of mint and cumin in their vegetable plots to make sure they kept the law that said they should give a tenth of all their produce to God.

If the eleventh commandment for Evangelical Christians is, "Thou shalt witness", then "Thou shalt tithe" has to be the twelfth. I don't want to knock tithing. The vast, world-changing social, evangelistic and missionary efforts which have sprung from the Evangelical sector of the Christian community would be impossible without the secure financial base that tithing provides. But, here again, we find an uncanny parallel with the Pharisees, as Jesus says,

> "Woe to you, teachers of the law and Pharisees, you hypocrites! you give a tenth of your spices – mint and dill and cummin. But you have neglected the more important matters of the law – justice, mercy and faithfulness. You should have practised the latter, without neglecting the former.
>
> (Matthew 23 v 23)

The original purpose of the law of the tithe was, to quote God's word through Malachi, "that there may be food in my House." Food tithed by the Israelites was stockpiled in the temple. This created a reserve from which the priests and Levites could live comfortably with enough left over to feed people in need and to provide for the enormous national parties which took place in the temple at pilgrim festivals, when Israelites gathered from all over the country to celebrate. The result of the tithe was a display of God's generosity, an exhibition of his care for his servants, and of the bond of brotherhood that held his people together. The Pharisees kept the law concerning tithing – to the letter. But they had lost sight of the reason for it. Their attitude to the poor was less than generous. They were willing to let injustices continue, so long as the letter of the law was being kept.

And again, their basic attitude was "how little can we get away with?" rather than "how much can we give" and "how can we protect those who are disadvantaged and needy?"

There are Christians who tithe as a matter of principle, but don't question the fact that Christian workers supposedly "supported" by the church are struggling to make ends meet. Like the Pharisees, Evangelical Christians, although hot on tithing, have traditionally tended to be less concerned than they could be with issues of injustice and poverty. In fairness this has changed dramatically over the last half century thanks to the efforts of organisations like Tearfund and World Vision. Even so, Evangelical involvement in social and political issues has traditionally tended to be limited to opposing pornography, abortion, and Sunday trading. It would be an unfair exaggeration to say that Evangelical Christians have been inactive in issues such as homelessness, unemployment and the injustices of international trade. That would be unfair to the many Evangelical Christians who have given time and effort to political and social initiatives in those areas. Even so, the accusation that they tithe, but show little concern for the "weightier matters of the law" is unfortunately true of many Evangelicals. Jesus says to them, as to the Pharisees: "You should have practised the latter, without neglecting the former."

Fifth Woe – Self-centred morality

Jesus went on to castigate the Pharisees about another of their failings:

> "Woe to you, teachers of the law and Pharisees, you hypocrites! You clean the outside of the cup and dish, but inside they are full of greed and self-indulgence. Blind Pharisee! First clean the inside of the cup and dish, and then the outside also will be clean."
>
> (Matthew 23 v 25–26)

There were rules in the Old Testament about cleaning utensils used for eating. There were certain foods which it was unlawful to eat (pork is the most well-known example). It wasn't so much a matter of hygiene as we would understand it. God had forbidden them to eat those foods and to eat them was to disobey God. Disobeying God meant that they could be excluded temporarily from the community. That meant they couldn't present themselves at the synagogue or temple for prayer or to offer sacrifices. By carefully cleaning the inside and outside of utensils used in drinking or eating, they could make sure that no trace of any forbidden substance contaminated any of the surfaces.

I think Jesus is using the words "inside" and "outside" in a special way here. "Outside" means the visible surfaces of the utensil, whether concave, convex or flat. The "inside" refers more to what they were used for and the way that they were used. The Pharisees were very careful about the physical cleanness of cups and dishes. But they used those same dishes and cups for banquets where people would get drunk and overeat in a totally selfish way, without regard for the needs of the poor. Some of the food and drink they consumed may also have been obtained or paid for by dishonest means.

Concern for hygiene today may have a more scientific basis. But it is still possible for us to be scrupulous in the way we do the washing up and yet have no conscience at all about where our food comes from, how it is obtained, whether those who produce it are treated fairly, and how self-indulgent we are in the way we consume it.

Sixth Woe – Righteousness without purity of heart

In a similar vein, Jesus continued,

> "Woe to you, teachers of the law and Pharisees, you hypocrites! You are like whitewashed tombs, which look beautiful on the outside, but on the inside are full of the bones of the dead and everything unclean. In the same way, on the outside you appear to people as righteous but on the inside you are full of hypocrisy and wickedness." (Matthew 23 v 27–28)

Many Christians instinctively assume that the correct Christian response to lawlessness and unrighteousness is to lift their voices in protest and disapproval. Unfortunately, most people in our semi-Christian society have, somewhere in the back of their minds, a dim memory that Jesus once said: "Let he who is without sin among you cast the first stone." They also know that those who profess to be Christians often fall short of their own ideals. They instinctively sense the hypocrisy of a church which sins and at the same time protests at the sins of others. In the same way the ordinary people who listened to Jesus instinctively sensed the hypocrisy of the Pharisees, who set themselves up as the guardians of morality in their day. What ordinary people in Jesus' day were looking for, and what ordinary people are still looking for today, is sincerity. It can be the sincere integrity of someone like Jesus who is as good on the inside as on the outside, or the sincere honesty of someone who openly admits their own weaknesses and failings, but keeps trying. They are looking, not for hypocrites to condemn them, but honest people who will model real goodness for them and help them achieve it. Jesus didn't need to condemn sin. His own goodness exposed it. So will ours, to the degree that we allow him to work through us.

Seventh Woe – Tradition without passion

Catholic and Orthodox churches have their saints. Evangelical Christianity also has its heroes – not prayed to and revered in the same way but held in honour, nevertheless: Martin Luther and John Calvin, the puritans, and great social reformers and missionaries. Each denomination reveres significant leaders from past generations: John and Charles Wesley for Methodists, William Carey and Charles Spurgeon for Baptists, William Booth for the Salvation Army, Smith Wigglesworth for Pentecostals, and so on. The Pharisees in Jesus' day had their heroes of the past too. Jesus said:

> "Woe to you, teachers of the law and Pharisees, you hypocrites. You build tombs for the prophets and decorate the graves of the righteous. And you say, 'If we had lived in the days of our forefathers, we would not have taken part with them in shedding the blood of the prophets.' So you testify against yourselves that you are the descendants of those who murdered the prophets."
> (Matthew 23 v 29–31)

It is easy to identify prophets, saints and heroes of the faith with hindsight. Recognising them in the present is not so easy. Sometimes they are uncomfortable to live with because they live according to God's agenda rather than ours, and they expose our unrighteousness and mediocrity. It is easy too, to honour their faith and courage, and bask in the second-hand glory of being their physical or spiritual descendants, without imitating their faith.

One of my favourite quotations is this:

> "Let us take from the altar of the past the fire and not the ashes."

These words are attributed to a French Socialist leader called Jean Jaurès but contain wisdom that applies just as much to faith as to politics.

To take only the ashes from the altar of the past means that we rigidly follow the traditions that our forebears handed down to us. In Christian terms, we run the church the way they did. If they baptised by immersion we do the same. If they venerated saints, we follow suit. If they prayed facing East, we pray facing East as well. If they worshipped with organ music we ban all other instruments from our services. We sanctify their way of doing things and make sure it stays the same for ever and never changes.

But taking the fire from the altar of the past means that we share the concerns that motivated our heroes of the past and imitate their courage and faith. If they sought to model their lives according to God's word, we do the same. We may come to different conclusions about the way to interpret the Bible but we imitate their courage by following our conscience and God's word whatever others say. We may not do exactly the same as them but, like them, we are prepared to swim against the tide and take risks in breaking new ground. If they sought to make the gospel relevant to their generation, we seek to make it relevant to ours. This may lead us to use different music and different methods, but our aim is the same as theirs was. Christians so often end up imitating the Pharisees. They think they are defending the tradition handed down to them by the prophets of the past, when what they are really doing is imitating the bigotry and prejudice of those who opposed the tradition before it became one.

A sting in the tail

Jesus' seven-fold condemnation of the Pharisees could hardly have been more thorough. But he rounded it off with an amazing piece of invective, a final sting in the tail of his thorough condemnation:

> "You snakes! You brood of vipers! How will you escape being condemned to hell? Therefore I am sending you prophets and sages and teachers. Some of them you will kill and crucify; others you will flog in your synagogues and pursue from town to town. And so upon you will come all the righteous blood that has been shed on earth, from the blood of righteous Abel to the blood of Zechariah son of Berakiah, whom you murdered between the temple and the altar." (Matthew 23 v. 33–36)

Here once again Jesus uses the image of snakes to point out the Pharisees' true motivation. The Pharisees are like little Satans. Like Satan they cast doubt on God's grace. Like Satan, they are out to accuse and condemn. The Pharisee emphasis on self-effort and adherence to the law as a path to salvation is not just wrong, it is a Satanically inspired corruption of the truth. Satan designed it to lead people into relying on their own righteousness so they fail to come under God's rule and so forfeit the benefits of the Kingdom in this life and eternal life in the age to come. Since, as we have noted, there is such an uncanny similarity between Pharisee religion and much that goes by the name of Christianity today, we need to sit up and take notice. Can it be that, right in the pulpits and pews of our churches are people who, albeit unintentionally, are doing Satan's work for him?

If you want to hide, the best place to hide is the place where people are least likely to expect you to be. Christians expect to find Satan frequenting sex-shops and new-age bookstores, and he knows that only too well. No doubt he has a hand in such establishments, but the trouble with open and obvious error is that it is open and obvious. There is too much danger of people realising that they are wrong, and repenting.

Satan is no fool. He knows that most decently brought up people are not going to be tempted overnight into being mass murderers or bank robbers or pimps. However, if he can convince people that they are being good and holy and righteous while he drags them to hell, he's on to a winner.

There are differing views among Christians as to the extent of demonic activity, and it is fashionable to denigrate those who "see demons round every corner". However, many Christians involved in the healing ministry are realising that the demonic realm is real and complex. Some Christians argue vehemently that a Christian can never have a demon. Others are open to the possibility that even professing Christians can be partly "demonised". Among those who hold this view and who have had experience of "deliverance" ministry, some profess to have come across "religious" spirits, who specialise in undercover operations, staying close to the faithful in religious settings in order to corrupt true religion and lead the saints into error. They speak of religious spirits, spirits of fanaticism, seducing spirits and spirits of corruption, along with, guess what: Pharisee spirits.

I will deal more fully with this aspect of Pharisaism in a later chapter, but whatever one thinks of this approach, the fact is that, at its root, Pharisaism is a Satanically inspired deceit. It is deceptively close to the truth, and yet so far from true Christianity – so plausible in using fine-sounding religious words like "holiness", "commitment" and "righteousness", and yet so far from the real spirit of Jesus.

I have majored on Pharisaism among Evangelicals, but I hasten to repeat that you will find Pharisees in every Christian tradition. You will find Anglo Catholic and Roman Catholic Pharisees, Greek Orthodox Pharisees and Liberal Non-Conformist Pharisees. What they share is first, the belief that we have to do something to gain acceptance with God, and secondly a peculiar kind of spiritual pride that comes from the deception that they are better than others, because they have passed the tests that others have failed.

Matthew doesn't tell us how the Pharisees responded to Jesus taking them apart in this way. They obviously had nothing to say in response. Jesus had decisively won yet another round in the conflict. But it wasn't over yet.

Chapter eleven

The Showdown

The Pharisees' hostility to Jesus had grown to the extent that they now wanted to get rid of him. Tragically, their motivation, in part at least, was love for God. It wasn't on their own account that they wanted to kill Jesus. In their mind Jesus was a blasphemer who insulted and misrepresented the Almighty and had to be stopped. They were trying to do God's will – and yet they were planning to kill God's only begotten Son in the process – an illustration of how disastrous the results can be when people try to do God's work for him. They should have known that God was powerful enough to defend his own interests. If they thought God needed them to fight his battles for him, then they were the ones who were misrepresenting God, not Jesus. Nevertheless, the Pharisees sincerely believed that God's purposes were best served by arranging for Jesus of Nazareth to die.

However, they faced the difficulty that they needed either a legal reason to have Jesus executed, or an opportunity to manipulate someone else into doing it for them in a way which would leave them with no blood on their hands. It was also essential that they had the authorities on their side, so that there would be no-one to accuse them of wrongdoing. Unfortunately, in First Century Judea, authority was a complicated issue.

The ultimate authority in the Jewish Community was the Sanhedrin. This council of 71 leaders met at the Temple in Jerusalem, and held considerable political and economic power within the provinces of Judea and Galilee. The Sanhedrin had two functions; it acted as a judiciary body, but it also had the kind of powers which might be held today by local or regional government – say by a county council in Britain. It existed only by the sufferance of the occupying Roman administration.

As long as the taxes were paid to Rome, the Romans allowed the Jews to manage their own affairs, within certain restrictions. One of those restrictions was that only the Romans could carry out the death penalty. In order to get rid of Jesus legally, therefore, the Pharisees had to provide reasons for executing Jesus that were covered in both Jewish and Roman law. They then had to convince the rest of the Sanhedrin, and then the Roman governor, that to have Jesus killed would be legally proper, politically advisable, and forensically justified.

There is plenty of evidence to indicate that it was the Pharisees who were the driving force behind the movement to have Jesus killed. As we have seen, they had a motive, in their belief that Jesus was leading people to abandon the law. They also had more to lose from Jesus' growing popularity among the ordinary people than anyone else did.

The Pharisee movement was essentially a grassroots movement. It had considerable support among the general population, but lacked representation in high places. Jesus' growing popularity meant that the Pharisees' own support-base was being threatened. The Sadducees had never had the same general support and drew most of their following from influential landowners and political leaders, so they were content to look on Jesus in a more benign way. It is unlikely that the Sadducees would have taken action against Jesus without encouragement from the Pharisees. In addition to all this, Jesus had publicly humiliated the Pharisees on several occasions. The Pharisees thus had theological, political and emotional reasons for opposing him.

The first hurdle they had to overcome was that of winning the Sanhedrin to their way of thinking. The Sanhedrin consisted of three groups of people: chief priests, scribes and elders. The chief priests represented the temple, and the sacrificial system. Of particular note among them was the High Priest, who tended to be regarded as the ultimate leader of the Jews, in the absence of a king (King Herod's jurisdiction covered Galilee and some other areas, but not Judea). The scribes were more than just expert writers. Copying the scriptures was an important part of their role but they were also theologians – experts in the Old Testament scriptures, especially the Law of Moses. The final group, the elders, consisted of influential heads of families. Although the Pharisees were well represented among the scribes, and the lower levels of the priesthood, the more senior priests and the elders belonged mainly to the Sadducee party. This is why the Pharisees needed to gain Sadducee support to arrange Jesus' death.

Once they had the support of the Sanhedrin, however, there remained the problem of persuading the Roman Governor. To persuade all these people that it was right to have Jesus killed was no easy task. It would be comparable to the opposition party in the British government setting out to persuade the government, the Confederation of British Industry and the leaders of all the main churches to lend their support to a decision which most of the population would oppose and which would need to be ratified by the President of the USA before it could be carried out. The combination of power bases involved in Jesus' trial and execution made it unlikely that the Pharisees would get all the agreements they needed, yet they apparently set themselves to pull all the strings needed to bring all the necessary people to their way of thinking.

Throughout the accounts of Jesus' arrest and trial it is the Chief Priests and the Sanhedrin who are to the fore, but John's Gospel gives the clue to the machination by the Pharisees which went on in the background. John wrote:

> "Therefore, many of the Jews who had come to visit Mary, and had seen what Jesus did, believed in him. But some of them went to the Pharisees and told them what Jesus had done. Then the chief priests and *the Pharisees* called a meeting of the Sanhedrin." (John 11 v 45–47, my emphasis)

We can deduce from what John says here that at some point a meeting took place between representatives of the Pharisee party and some or all of the chief priests. The priests had a vested interest in people keeping the law of Moses, since their livelihood and stature in the community depended on people observing the laws to do with tithing and sacrifice. It is easy to see how some of Jesus' statements, taken out of context, could have caused concern for the priests: "I desire mercy, not sacrifice," seemed to minimise the importance of sacrifices, for instance, and "Destroy this temple and in three days I will raise it up" could have been taken as a threat against the temple, as could "See these stones, not one will be left standing upon another."

Having won over the most influential priests, the Pharisees were then able to join them in calling a meeting of the whole Sanhedrin. At this meeting the proposal must have been put forward that Jesus should be arrested and judicially executed. It was evidently necessary for the Pharisees to use some persuasion, since not even all of their own number were in agreement. The New Testament records at least one dissenting voice, that of Nicodemus. According to John 11 v 48 the Chief Priest and the Pharisees used a lever to persuade the opposition. They hinted that, if they allowed Jesus to continue His ministry unchecked, the Romans would remove the limited self-rule that the Jews were allowed. This threat played to the deepest fears of the Sadducee rulers and obviously carried a lot of weight with them.

Once the members of the Sanhedrin had taken the decision to have Jesus executed, he was a marked man. He continued to appear in public, during the daylight hours, surrounded by a growing band of disciples (between seventy-two and one hundred and twenty in number) and a much larger crowd of less-committed enthusiasts. But Jesus kept his whereabouts at night-time secret. This created a further problem for his enemies. They could not arrest Him in the daytime without the risk of causing a riot, which in turn might precipitate a sudden, heavy-handed clampdown by the Romans. On the other hand, they didn't know where to find Jesus after dark.

It seems that a financial reward was offered for information as to Jesus' whereabouts at night and it may have been this that prompted Judas Iscariot to make his offer to lead the authorities to where Jesus could be found. When Judas came to meet Jesus in the garden of

Gethsemane, John specifically mentions that some officials from the Chief Priests and the Pharisees were with him.

The Pharisees may have needed the support of other power bases to help them bring about Jesus' execution, and the decision may have rested with others – the Sanhedrin, the Chief Priests, and the Roman Governor – but the Pharisees were there in the background, stirring others up and keeping the momentum going until Jesus was dealt with.

After Jesus' crucifixion Matthew specifically mentions that it was the Pharisees who came to Pilate with some of the Chief Priests to ask for the tomb to be sealed:

> "The next day, the one after Preparation Day, the chief priests and the Pharisees went to Pilate. 'Sir,' they said, 'we remember that this deceiver said, "After three days I will rise again." So give the order for the tomb to be made secure until the third day. Otherwise his disciples may come and steal the body and tell the people that he has been raised from the dead...' "
>
> (Matthew 27 v 62–64).

It is a measure of the way in which Jesus had got "under the skin" of the Pharisees that, even after bringing about his death, they were still wanting to give expression to their anger and disapproval. Killing him wasn't enough; they wanted to make sure his body was firmly boxed up and shut away. Maybe deep down they had a secret fear that he was who he hinted he was – the promised Messiah, the very Son of God. They seemed to be still afraid of Jesus, even after he had been killed. The petty, feeble action of sealing the tomb reveals the real issue at stake in Pharisaism. If Jesus was an ordinary man, there was no need for a seal on the tomb. But if Jesus was from God, what they were trying to do was to restrain and restrict God's power, to "box God in". Pharisaism is an attempt to achieve God's approval by human effort, but the fact is that God's approval can only be won by acknowledging the insufficiency of human effort, and our total dependence on him. Pharisaism looks like holiness, but in fact it is an attempt to usurp God's authority and power – to come alongside God as a peer, instead of acknowledging him as one before whom we are all nothing.

In the Pharisee's eyes, Jesus was a sinner. That's why they condemned him to die. To them He was a law breaker and a blasphemer. Mind you, there was a lot of rationalisation going on there. Personal motives lay below the surface. Jesus had made them look silly, and he had undermined their security. Resentment paraded as righteousness as they campaigned for his death.

Uncannily, the urge to condemn and disapprove is not quenched by the ultimate disapproval and condemnation of death. You can be angry enough to kill someone, but killing them doesn't rid you of the anger. In a typical Pharisee pattern, the Pharisees continued to give expression to their rejection of the "sinner" (as they judged Jesus to be), even after the need had been exhausted by his death. Only mercy can bring the inward peace and satisfaction that justice and resentment crave. Pharisees can never come to a place of real peace.

There is a lesson to be learned here which is applicable to divisions that occur in churches in the present day. When we find ourselves in disagreement with someone, or hurt, irritated or offended by them, our immediate gut reaction tends to be like that of the Pharisees to Jesus. We want them out of the way and dealt with. We may not resort to violence and murder, outwardly, but our inward motive may be very similar – the desire to remove that person from the situation – to "kill them off", so they are no longer a cause of frustration or pain to us. Even if we follow the path of political manoeuvring to oust them or we simply ignore that person and give them the cold-shoulder until they go away, we are choosing the Pharisee approach rather than doing things Jesus' way.

Chapter twelve

Beware the Leaven of the Pharisees

We began by noting how Jesus and the Pharisees seem, at first sight, to be very close in their outlook and aims. The Pharisees shared with Jesus a deep reverence for God, a total respect for the Old Testament Scriptures, an openness to the supernatural world, and a radical approach to righteousness. But as we have come to see, the differences are far reaching. The diagram below summarises what these differences are.

Pharisees	**Jesus**
Judge the action.	Judges the motivation.
View the law as an end in itself.	Views the law as a means to maintain relationships.
Lived to condemn.	Died to save.
See the motive for goodness as to gain approval.	Sees the motive for goodness as being to glorify God.

On one occasion Jesus warned his disciples:

> "Be on your guard against the yeast of the Pharisees, which is hypocrisy" (Luke 12 v 1)

Comparing the different accounts of this saying in the synoptic gospels shows that the three writers had different ideas about the precise words that Jesus spoke here. However, all three agree that he particularly singled out the Pharisees in this warning. In Matthew Jesus warns against "the yeast of the Pharisees and the Sadducees". In Mark He refers to "the yeast of the Pharisees and Herod". In Luke He just mentions the Pharisees. "Leaven" was a piece of dough which was kept back and fermented so as to be used to start the fermentation process in a new loaf. We use yeast to produce the same effect today. That's why some translations say "leaven" and others say "yeast".

Both Matthew and Mark say that this statement by Jesus occurred soon after the feeding of the five thousand. Before this miracle took place there had been a discussion in which some of the disciples had pressurised Jesus to send the crowd away to get food. Jesus had insisted to the disciples that they should provide food for the crowd themselves. This conversation evidently left the disciples thinking that Jesus had expected them to have the foresight to provide food for the crowd beforehand and that by not doing so they had let him down. They were left feeling that Jesus had performed the miracle to get them off the hook after a massive piece of incompetence. They thought that he had expected them to arrange for the crowds who had come to listen to him to be fed. They were left feeling that, if they had been efficient disciples they would have made careful plans and arranged for caterers to be on hand, so that the miracle would have been unnecessary.

When Jesus began to talk about "leaven" or "yeast", it triggered a chain of mental associations in their minds which reminded them of bread and their failure to provide food for the crowds. Their thoughts went something like this:

> "Yeast – bread – oh, no – we forgot, again! Don't worry, Jesus, we'll see to it right away! We're so sorry! Someone will go off

> and order it... when do you want it delivered? How much should we get? Do we give it away, or get people to pay?"

Jesus has to stop them and bring their thoughts back to the point he is really making. He is not talking about ordering bread. He has already proved that He can provide bread, whenever they need it. Providing bread is not a problem. He is simply using an analogy of the effect of leaven, or yeast, in bread to warn them against the effect of the Pharisees' teaching. A little bit of it can spread and grow, and affect the whole lump of dough. Later on, a noted ex-Pharisee, Paul, was to use the same analogy to illustrate the effect of sin within a church community (see I Corinthians 5 v 8).

One thing is certain and that is that Jesus definitely warned the first disciples against the pervasive, corrupting effect of the teaching of the Pharisees. The leaven stands as a symbol of corruption. Jesus regarded the Pharisees' teaching as a corruption of the truth which was so dangerous in its effects that he took care to warn us against it. Like leaven it spreads and affects the whole lump. Not only is it in many ways the antithesis of the Good News that Jesus came to proclaim, its effects on us can be destructive in the extreme. Pharisaism prevents us from enjoying God's grace and experiencing the power of the Holy Spirit. Worse, it can rob us of our eternal salvation by drawing us back into relying on right works or right ideas as the basis of our present life and future hope, rather than simple trust in the provision he has made for our forgiveness through the death of his Son.

In view of this it is amazing to look back from a twentieth century vantage point over two thousand years of Christian history and to see how Pharisaism has been a problem in the Christian community in every generation – even from the very beginning. Within a few years of Jesus' ascension, the Church had trouble with Judaisers who tried to introduce a basically Pharisaical outlook into a Christian framework.

Even the apostle Peter had a struggle against the Pharisee within him. God had to help him through a dream to get over his Pharisaical prejudices and go to preach the gospel in the home of Cornelius, a gentile. As he preached to the people gathered there, God had to make sure that those who heard were baptised in the Holy Spirit and spoke in tongues before Peter had the chance to demand they should be circumcised first. Later on, Paul needed to rebuke Peter for slipping back into Pharisee ways (see Galatians 22 v 11 ff.). From the time the gospel began to spread to Gentiles in Antioch, there were Jewish Christians who maintained that the Gentiles needed to submit to circumcision in order to be acceptable to God. Acts 15 v 5 refers to these people as believers who belonged to the party of the Pharisees. This implies that there were Pharisees who acknowledged Jesus as Messiah, and who submitted to baptism, yet continued their connection with the Pharisee movement, without seeing any conflict between the two loyalties. In his letters, Paul makes constant reference to Christians who are going back to relying on keeping rules and regulations, and relying on the law instead of on grace and faith.

As time went on, the Pharisee influence continued to work away like leaven in the life of the church. The name disappeared, so did the strict adherence to every detail of the law of Moses, but the basic approach remained and found expression in observance of new laws as a way to salvation. By the sixteenth century this Pharisaical influence had begun to predominate to the extent that preachers were promising people they could earn themselves a place in Heaven by making a contribution to the cost of a planned new cathedral in Rome. This was the starting point for the Reformation. Martin Luther's great re-discovery was that we are saved by faith in God's grace, not by human effort. The other great reformation leader, John Calvin, agreed, and emphasised that man is totally unable to make himself acceptable to God by his own efforts. He asserted that God is sovereign and salvation comes solely by God's grace and power, not by our puny efforts at self-righteousness.

And what about the church today? The leaven of the Pharisees is remarkably persistent and is still having its effect. Wherever there is reliance on human effort and goodness rather than the grace of God, wherever Christians judge others by their actions without examining the motives behind those actions, wherever Christians are more concerned to protest than to proclaim, more eager to condemn the lost than to reclaim them, wherever adherence to "the law" (God's or ours) is demanded as a condition of acceptance rather than encouraged as a response to God's mercy, there you have the leaven of the Pharisees, still working its way through the dough of the Christian Church, spreading its corruption.

But why is Pharisaism so persistent? There are a number of reasons but I would suggest three that are of particular note. These are:

- Human personality;
- The desire to be in control; and
- The effect of religious demonic spirits.

Let's look at each in turn:

Human personality

All of us are vulnerable to Pharisaism but some people are more predisposed towards Pharisaism because of their personality. A combination of their genetic make up and formative experiences in their lives makes these people more prone to a Pharisee outlook than others. The contrast between a road vehicle and a railway train provides a useful way to understand their vulnerability. Motor vehicles are free to weave in and out of the traffic and even drive on the wrong side of the road, if occasion demands. Railway trains, on the other hand, cannot function without tracks laid down for them to run on.

Some people feel secure and confident when they have a set of rules which act like railway lines to keep them on track. The tracks laid down liberate them from the constant pressure of making decisions. When they have rules they have direction and security but they will experience stress and anxiety if you put them in a situation where there are no rules to follow or where other people ignore or undermine the rules that there are.

Other people, in contrast, feel that rules stifle their creativity and hem them in. They are able to cope without rules by considering the probable outcomes of various possible actions and then making appropriate choices. They feel energised and excited by the fluidity that comes as they respond moment by moment to an ever-changing situation.

These differences can be explained as part of the well known Myers Briggs system, which is one of the most widely accepted approaches to personality analysis. Myers Briggs categorises people according to their position on a set of four axes:

Extrovert – Introvert (E – I)
Sensing – Intuitive (S – N)
Thinking – Feeling (T – F)
Judging – Perceiving (J – P)

People are assigned to various personality types indicated by a sequence of four letters – for example, when I had a Myers Briggs analysis, I came out as an INFJ. That means that:

- I draw my strength from within myself rather than from other people (I)
- I am intuitive, seeing the bigger picture rather than concentrating on the detail (N)
- I am motivated by feelings (F)
- I take an analytical, judging approach to problems (J).

Someone who is the exact opposite of me would be an ESTP:

- Drawing strength from relationships with others (E)
- Concentrating on the detail (S)
- Driven by logic rather than emotion (T).
- Making decisions based on experience rather than analysis (P)

It is interesting to try to fit typical Pharisee tendencies into the Myers Briggs framework. Those who are by nature sensing, thinking and judging, with the letters S, T or J as part of their personality type, will have elements of the "railway train" mentality. They will feel comfortable following a set of rules which have a logical foundation.

Introverts will tend to stick to the rules for fear of exposure and the disapproval of their peers.

Sensing people will stick to the rules because that's what they were taught to do.

Thinking people will stick to the rules because not to do so would bring unacceptable consequences.

The Judging person will stick to the rules because that gives them a sense of security. Pharisaism will thus come quite easily to an ISTJ personality, and anyone with S,T or J, tendencies will be prone to slip into some aspects of the Pharisee outlook.

Only the ENFP personality can hope to be free from Pharisee tendencies to any large extent. The nearer you come to that extreme, the more open you will be to "cutting corners" or "bending the rules" to reach a desired objective and hence you will be less likely to have Pharisee tendencies. However, that means that you will be more prone to the opposite danger of being too lawless and undisciplined. The Myers Briggs categories explain tendencies; they don't absolve us from responsibility of our actions.

Neuroses also have a play to play in making people more or less likely to follow the Pharisee path. Neuroses are personality tendencies identified by psychiatrists and distinguished from psychoses. Psychoses are forms of mental illness where people lose contact with reality and experience delusions. Neuroses are less pronounced psychological tendencies where people don't lose contact with reality but nevertheless struggle with inner urges that pull them in unhelpful directions. Neuroses include mild depression, anxiety, obsessive-compulsive disorders and the "hysterical" personality which needs constant affirmation and attention to combat inner insecurities. As many as twenty per cent of the population at any time are likely to be suffering from some kind of neurosis, if only in a mild form. Several neurotic tendencies can be associated with a tendency towards Pharisaism in a religiously motivated person.

The obsessive-compulsive person for instance, will be afraid of breaking rules. The hysterical personality may find it hard to resist the rules laid down by authority figures and be afraid of being rejected if they break them. A depressive person will have high standards and be convinced that they are not good enough. Again, neurotic tendencies only explain a bias. They don't remove a person's responsibilitty for their actions.

The desire to be in control

Personality types and neuroses may make some people more prone to Pharisaical behaviour but, leaving personality types and neuroses aside, all of us – whatever our personality or psychiatric condition – feel more secure when we are in control of our own destiny.

That is the attraction of Pharisaical religion – it puts us in the driving seat. It offers us the hope of achieving goodness, and rewards us if we do. It tells us that we can manipulate God into favouring us if we do what pleases him. Furthermore, being able to look down on others who have failed, or broken the rules, boosts our own sense of self worth. On the other hand, to admit that you are a fallen creature with an inherited tendency towards sin, who is incapable of reaching the standard of complete righteousness, and is totally dependent on God's mercy for everything, can be scary, even though in the long run it brings the truest and most lasting joy.

All this would be enough to explain the persistence of Pharisaism, but in addition, I believe, there is a deeper and more sinister level which we should not ignore.

Religious demonic spirits

One of the most noticeable aspects of Jesus' ministry was the way he cast evil spirits out of people who were afflicted in various ways. How do we respond to this aspect of Jesus' ministry? It has become fashionable to ignore it, assuming that Jesus was merely accommodating his approach to the simplistic and superstitious world view of the time and that this practice has no relevance to our culture today. However, this view is so full of inconsistencies that it is logically untenable:

1. If Jesus had come as the Son of God to reveal the truth, why should he accommodate his approach to a worldview that was untrue?
2. If demons were not the real cause of people's problems, why did Jesus not simply deal with the real causes and let the results speak for themselves?

3. If Jesus is our example and role model, how can we pick and choose which bits of his life we imitate and which we filter out?

The consistent witness of the synoptic gospels is that Jesus cast out demons. All four gospels present Jesus' life in terms of a conflict with an unseen, demonic enemy. If that is the case, and the Pharisees were involved in bringing about Jesus' death, it is impossible to escape the implication that the Pharisees were motivated by demons (albeit without knowing it). If we are to truly follow Jesus seriously, we need to take demons seriously too. If the life of Jesus was a constant conflict with a demonic enemy, we have to be open to the possibility that his death was brought about by that enemy.

I realise that this subject is controversial and many readers will find it hard to accept, but if you fall into this category I would ask you to bear with me and weigh and judge what I say for yourself. I have already noted the experience of some Charismatic Christians involved in the deliverance ministry who claim to have encountered "religious spirits", including a category of Pharisee spirits whose brief is to twist and corrupt Christians in order to turn them away from the grace of God. I want to make it clear here that I am not talking about spirit "possession" in the popular sense. In the Bible spirits never possess people, it is always the other way round – people "have" spirits or are "demonised", (The 16th century expression "possessed of", found in the Authorised King James Bible, has caused the misunderstanding which is responsible for the erroneous popular view of possession).

It is relatively easy to accept that demons may be involved in occult religious practices such as witchcraft or necromancy or fortune telling, or even to admit the possibility that those who indulge in persistent sin may open themselves to demonic influence. It is understandably more difficult to come to terms with the idea that practising Christians might need "deliverance" and that demonic spirits might be at work in the midst of Christian activity and even in services of worship. Until experience led me to re-examine the scriptures, I would have agreed with those who say it is impossible for the Holy Spirit and a demon to exist side by side in one person. I now believe there is another framework of understanding which fits Scripture and human experience better.

Jesus called Satan 'The Prince of this world' (see John 12 v 31). Human society is to a degree under Satan's control. Satan influences human society through the work of his army of rebellious angels. The sin which exists in each of us has its source in demonic temptation. This doesn't remove our personal responsibility, because we have the power and the duty to resist. Nevertheless, temptation is more than just a combination of human desire and the opportunity to fulfil it. There is a third level involved in temptation, involving demonic oppression or enticement. When you give in to temptation you yield a degree of control over one aspect of your life to the demons which have been oppressing you. This may result in demons gaining a stronghold of power in one aspect of your behaviour.

Through his death on the cross, Jesus purchased for each of us freedom from guilt and thus the right to be freed from demonic control. By trusting in Jesus we become his by right, and are given the power of the Holy Spirit to resist Satan. The Holy Spirit takes up residence within us, uniting with our human spirit. However, this does not immediately remove the demonic influence from within our souls and bodies. We now have the right to remove demons from their strongholds in our lives and the power to resist their activity, but we still have to use our position of authority and power to remove them bit by bit, through a life of continual and continuing repentance. What is normally referred to now as "deliverance ministry" may play a significant part in this process. The Holy Spirit does not eject demonic spirits for us. He empowers us to do it. If we are double-minded and less than determined in our renunciation of sin, we give demons the right to remain. A person in this situation is a walking battlefield. This isn't what God wants for us, but practically, it is the situation in which most Christians find themselves today. Paradoxically, a double-minded Christian may actually be more prone to sin than an unbeliever, because Satan will be more eager to oppose the work of the Holy Spirit in someone who has leanings towards goodness than in someone who has no desire for goodness at all.

Rather than Satan's activity being limited to obviously evil places, a central part of his strategy is to destroy, divide, discredit or divert the church. If the Holy Spirit and demonic spirits can exist within different parts of one person, how much more so within a whole organisation?

When you go to church, you can expect to meet God, but be aware that you will also encounter Satan. As is made clear in I Peter 5 v 8, the wolf or lion prowls around the sheepfold, because he knows that's where his prey are to be found.

This may explain why so many people end up disillusioned with the church and disappointed by its failures – why so many churches are rent apart by power struggles or compromised by immorality or materialism. Satan has a strategy. There are two kinds of Christian that he particularly targets: the strategic and the vulnerable. He expends a lot of effort to attack strategic leaders because he knows he can do damage through them as well as in them. He also attacks those who are weak in faith and vulnerable because he knows they are easy prey. How does he target them? Sometimes he seeks to entice them into obvious sin but the problem with overt wrongdoing, from Satan's point of view, is just that – it is too obvious. If he can entrap people and prevent them from enjoying God's grace while at the same time they are continuing to think of themselves as good Christians, he is succeeding (he's also happy for people to consider themselves as good Jews or Muslims or Buddhists – one legalistic religion is as good as another from his point of view).

Let me briefly lay out some of the Biblical evidence which supports this view.

Jesus prophesied that the time would come when false Messiahs and false prophets would deceive even the elect. How else could they do it if not through the activity of deceiving demonic spirits?

In I Timothy 4 v 1, Paul wrote:

> "The Spirit clearly says that in the later times some will abandon the faith and follow deceiving spirits and things taught by demons."

In I Thessalonians, he talked of a day when a "Man of lawlessness" will lead a "final rebellion" against God. He says that "the secret power of lawlessness" is already at work. In other words, there are tendencies already operating in the world which will one day become personified in one particular evil person. John gives this figure the name of "antichrist":

> "Dear children, this is the last hour; and as you have heard that the antichrist is coming, even now many antichrists have come."
> (1 John 2 v 18)

A big antichrist to come – but there are going to be many people in the meantime who display the qualities of antichrist, the result of a demonic spiritual power at work in them:

> "Every spirit that does not acknowledge Jesus is not from God. This is the spirit of the antichrist, which you have heard is coming and even now is already in the world." (1 John 4 v 3)

What can be more "anti-Christ" than a teaching that says that we don't need Jesus in order to be saved? Pharisaism is one aspect of the ruling spirit of antichrist. One day this ruling demonic spirit will come to a head in a specific personified form, but in the meantime, as John says, there are "many antichrists" in the form of people who claim to be Christians, and who sincerely believe they are Christians, yet who, under the influence of the spirit of antichrist, deny the very good news of mercy that Jesus came to bring. At the same time, many of us who really are Christians find ourselves tempted, as a result of the influence of the same evil spirit, to doubt and forget and slip back like the Galatians into trusting in our own right behaviour or right doctrine. This is the greatest danger that faces each Christian, and we need to be constantly on our guard against this pervasive "leaven of the Pharisees" which threatens to rob us of all Jesus died to obtain on our behalf.

We need to be aware that this is a spiritual battle, not just a matter of remembering to believe the right things. We need to single-mindedly put away from ourselves the desire to be self-reliant and in control of our spiritual destiny. We need to allow God to be God in our lives. Those of us who have a leaning towards Pharisaism by virtue of our personality need to be especially on guard.

There is only one sure antidote to the leaven of the Pharisees and that is to live constantly in the light of God's love for us. The more we understand his mercy and grace, the less we will feel the need to justify ourselves to him. Along with this we need to maintain a realistic openness to our human frailty and the selfishness which is central to every human being. The only way to remain immune to Pharisaical pride and self-reliance is to maintain an attitude of humble, yet joyful dependence on God. We can't even do that through our own self-effort. This humble attitude comes naturally as we hold on to the knowledge of three things:

- the fact that we have nothing in ourselves to commend us to God;
- the fact of God's unquenchable grace, and
- the sacrifice that Jesus made on our behalf at the cross.

Chapter thirteen

Born Again

One evening, Jesus received a surprising visitor. He came secretly, perhaps afraid of repercussions if it became known that he had been to visit Jesus. Nicodemus was an influential Pharisee, a member of the Sanhedrin, and a wealthy man. He had much to lose by being associated with Jesus – but something about the Galilean prophet stirred his interest enough to persuade him to set up and keep this risky after-dark appointment.

I imagine the two men facing each other in dim lamplight – Jesus relaxed, compassion showing in his eyes, as he gave his full attention to his guest; Nicodemus, tense and ill at ease, nervously clearing his throat as he began to speak:

> "Rabbi, we know you are a teacher who has come from God. For no-one could perform te signs you are doing if God were not with him …" (John 3 v 2)

Jesus interrupted him in mid-sentence. It is so obvious that the next word to come from Nicodemus' mouth was going to be "… but …"

> "… we know that you are a teacher who has come from God, for no-one could perform the miraculous signs you are doing if God were not with him, *but...*'

Jesus interrupted him before he spoke the "...but..." Nicodemus was about to raise an objection or ask a question about Jesus' ministry, and we shall never know what it was. We can make guesses. Perhaps he was going to say,

> "... but you don't seem to uphold the law – why is that?"

Maybe he was just going to say,

> "... but what's going on here? What does it mean?"

We don't know. Jesus may have guessed, or he may have known through the Holy Spirit what Nicodemus was about to say. If so, he evidently decided that what Nicodemus had already said was more important than what what was coming next, because he interrupted the Pharisee in midstream by picking up on the opening of his nicely rehearsed speech:

> "Very truly I tell you, no one can see the kingdom of God unless they are born again."

An unfortunate consequence of having the Bible divided into verses is that it is easy to isolate a verse from those before and after and so miss the connections between them. This is an example. What Jesus said was not an abrupt interruption, it was a response to what Nicodemus had already said. The little word "see" is the key – Nicodemus had seen something. He had seen miracles take place. He had seen the presence of God in Jesus. He had seen that Jesus was a teacher sent from God. Those were signs of the Kingdom of God breaking into human history and, more particularly, into Nicodemus' life. They were acts of God. Nicodemus had seen them, and drawn the right conclusions, so Jesus affirmed him. Not everyone had been so perceptive. Some had not seen what Nicodemus saw, or been unwilling to see it, or refused to believe their eyes. But Nicodemus had seen what was happening and was drawing the right conclusions. Jesus was impressed by this and so he responded by saying "Nicodemus, you would not have seen and understood what you have, unless you had been born again."

It is remarkable how powerful an effect one popular hymn can have on the thinking of the church. The whole Protestant world today shares an understanding of this verse which is slightly off-beam and owes a lot to a Victorian gospel song which became popular in the late 19th Century through a collection of hymns called *Sacred Songs and Solos*. The famous gospel singer Ira D. Sankey compiled this hymnbook for use in D.L. Moody's campaigns. It brought the musical style of the music hall into the church and remained popular well into the 20th century. One of the most popular songs in this collection is about Nicodemus' visit to Jesus. It had a chorus, repeated after each verse, which was taken from John 3 v 7 in the Authorised Version:

> "Ye must be born again, Ye must be born again,
> I verily, verily say unto you, Ye must be born again."

The rhythm of the song stressed the word "must".

Influenced in part by this song Evangelical preachers have, for more than a century, urged on their hearers the necessity of being born again. The phrase "born again" came to be used as another way of talking about "conversion" and the phrase "born again Christian" was coined to describe enthusiastic Christians of an Evangelical persuasion. More recently, the phrase "born again" has worked its way into the English language as a general term meaning "enthusiastic, dedicated, and slightly fanatical". However, the truth is that what Jesus said to Nicodemus was not "You must be born again," in the sense of something you must do yourself, but "You need to be born again, in the sense of something done to you." Jesus was stating a necessity, not issuing a command. He was not telling Nicodemus what he had to do, he was explaining what had happened to him already.

If Jesus had unpacked the statement he would have said something like, "You don't know it yet, Nicodemus, but something has happened to you. That's why you have seen what you have seen. Your awareness of God at work through me is evidence of the new birth that is already taking place in you."

Nicodemus, understandably, was puzzled by what Jesus said. Apart from the fact that the connection with what he was trying to say to Jesus wasn't obvious, what Jesus had said in his interruption didn't seem to make sense anyway. As Nicodemus observed, "How can a grown man be born again? He can't go back in his mother's womb and come out again, can he?" Furthermore, what Jesus had said was ambiguous. You could take it two different ways, because the word that is translated "again" can also mean "from above."

So Jesus began to explain. A person cannot enter the kingdom of God, He said, unless he is born over again/from above. This needs some explanation for the modern English reader. As we saw in a previous chapter, the word "kingdom" is not a particularly good translation of the Greek word *basileia* that Jesus used. In English a "kingdom" is what a king rules over, either people or territory. But *basileia* is slightly different. It means government by a king. It stands in the same category as words such as "administration", "government", "policy", and "strategy". It is what a king does, not what a king has. Jews had for centuries been waiting eagerly for the day when God would step into their national affairs and act in power. They looked forward to the day when God would come and sort things out. They expected that God would do it through a new king, but it would be God's act because, really, God alone was their king – human kings just represented him. When God stepped in and asserted his authority, evil would be defeated, wrongs would be put right and a new age would dawn. Everyone in the world would know that their God was the God. Every Jew longed to be alive to see that day and to experience the "Life of the age" (misguidingly translated "eternal life" or "everlasting life" in most English Bibles) – the joy of living under God's administration.

So what is Jesus saying here? He is saying several things:

First, and most significantly, he is saying that the time of the "kingdom" has begun. The King has come, and God is acting in power and authority through him.

Secondly, Jesus is saying that it is only possible to be aware of this fact – to see, or to discern what God is doing – if you first become the recipient of an act of God which is similar in effect to being born. A baby in the womb is alive, but knows only the inner world of the womb.

There is another world all around it, which it cannot see and in which it cannot participate. But once it has been born it sees and hears, and can become active itself in the wider world. In the same way the person who has not experienced the re-birth Jesus was speaking of, is unaware of the realm of the Spirit, unable to discern God's activity. But when the Holy Spirit brings them to spiritual rebirth, it is like breaking out of the darkness of the womb into a new world, where you see things to which you were previously blind.

Lastly, Jesus is saying that, without this experience of new birth, it is impossible to enter the realm of God's kingdom rule, to experience the kingdom of God. Jesus uses an analogy to help us understand what he wants to say here. He talks about the wind. Had he lived in a more modern age, he might just as easily have used electricity as an example. Both electricity, and the wind, are invisible. You can't see them, but you can see and feel the effects of their presence. You don't know where the wind came from, and you don't know where it's going to. But you do know it's there. People who are born again/born from above have a powerful force acting through them. You can compare the effects of it to those of the wind or electricity. You can't see it. Those people don't glow in the dark, or hum with energy – they look like everyone else. But something is evidently at work in them which makes them different. In fact, the something is a Someone – God Himself, who is working through them, establishing his rule in their lives, and using them to execute his rule in the world.

Nicodemus was quite correct in his observation that "no-one can enter his mother's womb a second time and be born". Birth is not something we have under our control. A baby doesn't conceive itself, cause itself to grow and then force its way out of the womb (it might seem like that to the mother, but the baby is as helpless a victim of nature as the mother herself in the process!). In the same way, none of us can decide to be born again. That's the error of the old Sankey hymn. It's no use saying "Ye *must* be born again," because it's as pointless as saying to a baby in the womb, "You really should get yourself born now!" Some translations do use the words "you must" in verse 7, but it isn't a command, but a statement of fact.

The Pharisees' approach to religion was an activist one. The Pharisees had a long list of "you musts" as well as an even longer list of "you must nots". If Jesus had simply added another obligation to the list: "Rule number 2001: you must be born again." Nicodemus could have easily fitted what Jesus said into his framework of understanding. Even if it was impossible, Nicodemus would have done his best to fulfil the new commandment. But Jesus was offering him something that was completely outside of his control – something done to him, not something he had to do. He wasn't used to thinking that way, and he had to struggle to understand it. Jesus was in the process of turning upside-down his whole way of thinking, believing and living.

As Jesus continued his explanation, he reminded Nicodemus of an incident in one of the books of Moses, with which he would have be familiar. The Israelites were being plagued by snakes. People were dying from the poison in the snake bites and God told Moses to make a bronze snake, and stick it up on a pole, high above the camp, so that wherever people were they could look at the pole. People who were bitten were to look at the snake on the pole and they would be healed.

Then Jesus did the most amazing thing. He predicted his own death. "I too," He said, "am going to be 'lifted up'." "Lifted up" was a euphemism for "crucified". Since crucifixion was a Roman practice, the Jews didn't have a word for it in their language. When the Romans crucified someone from the Jewish community the Jews would say to one another, "Did you hear what happened to poor so-and so? – the Romans lifted him up." And so Jesus said, "Just as the snake was lifted up on the pole, so I am going to be lifted up, and anyone who looks to me, who relies on me, will have the 'life of the age'. They will experience the Rule of God."

> "For God so loved the world that he gave his one and only Son, that whoever believes on him shall not perish but have eternal life. For God did not send his Son into the world to condemn the world, but to save the world through him. Whoever believes in him is not condemned but whoever does not believe stands condemned already because they have not believed in the name of God's one and only Son."
>
> (John 3 v 16–18)

As Jesus was speaking, Nicodemus must have been like someone trying to co-ordinate their hand movements while looking in a mirror. Jesus was showing him a view of the world which was back-to-front and upside-down, and he must have struggled to grasp it. The Pharisees were expecting that the arrival of the Kingdom of God would be primarily about condemnation. They saw it as the time when everyone who had failed morally or deliberately broken the law would get what they deserved. God would reveal their badness and remove them from the face of the earth so the good people could live in peace. Those who had tried hard and been good would enjoy the life of the age to come.

In contrast to this idea of the kingdom as a time of judgement, Jesus offered a vision of the Kingdom which was to do with mercy, rescue, and restoration – God giving people who had sinned an opportunity to be forgiven. All they had to do was to come to Jesus – look to Him –- trust in him. Even that action, to an extent, is involuntary. The looking and trusting is the result of the new birth, not a precondition of it. It is the Holy Spirit who brings people to the point of looking to Jesus in that way. Just as a physical birth has to be preceded by conception, the implantation of the father's seed into the mother, so spiritual birth begins with the sowing of seed. In several of his parables Jesus used the analogy of seed being sown, the seed being the message of the kingdom. The message itself produces the response in people. Some ignore it, others respond by just taking it in and believing.

John doesn't record Nicodemus' immediate response. My guess was that he politely thanked Jesus, and went off to think about it some more. But the seed had been sown in his mind, and Nicodemus was later the first Pharisee to become one of Jesus disciples. Further on in John's Gospel, we find Nicodemus using his influence among the Pharisees to protect Jesus. When some of them were pressing for Jesus to be assassinated, it was Nicodemus who prevented them from condemning Jesus without a trial. After Jesus' death, Nicodemus accompanied Joseph of Arimathea to see Pilate and to ask for Jesus' body to be released to them for burial; and the two secret disciples together attended to Jesus' burial. Almost certainly John obtained this information from Nicodemus himself, who probably went on to become a member of the early Christian Church.

There has to be a "probably" there because we do not know for certain that Nicodemus did come out and follow Jesus openly. However, we do know from the Acts of the Apostles that there were some Pharisees who became believers. Nicodemus may well have been one of them.

Luke's account of the early history of the Church in the Acts of the Apostles gives the impression that, after Jesus' crucifixion, it was the Sadducee party who caused the most trouble for the early Christian community and that the Pharisees had a change of heart, at least to some extent. Jesus' resurrection may well have had something to do with this. The Pharisees may not have personally seen Jesus after his resurrection, but they could not ignore the empty tomb, the story told by the guards who had been there and the rumours that people had seen Jesus alive. The Sadducees would have been eager to squash any talk of a resurrection, since the rumours undermined their "liberal" faith which had no place for the "paranormal" or "supernatural". The Pharisees, on the other hand, did believe in the resurrection of the dead, and many of them must have begun to wonder if the stories being told about Jesus' resurrection were true. So this may explain why we find one of the most influential Pharisees, Gamaliel, advocating a more *laissez faire* attitude to Christians;

> "I advise you, leave these men alone! Let them go! For if their purpose or activity is of human origin, it will fail. But if it is from God, you will not be able to stop these men; you will only find yourself fighting against God." (Acts 5 v 38-39).

Acts 15 v 5 refers to "Some of the believers who belonged to the party of the Pharisees". Evidently there were Pharisees who, without giving up their Pharisee allegiance and outlook, began to follow Jesus. They acknowledged Jesus as Messiah, they were baptised and began to experience the power of the Holy Spirit but their understanding of the Christian message was still: "If you have broken the law, God will forgive you, provided you trust in Jesus and keep the commandments." They simply added baptism and faith to their list of laws. They were still hoping to be "good enough" for God to accept them. They had joined the Christian church, accepted that Jesus was the Messiah, believed in the resurrection, but didn't fully grasp the core of Jesus' teaching. At heart they were still Pharisees.

The same pattern was repeated throughout the ancient world as the apostles spread the message, often making their first converts in each town from the local synagogue. There was a growing number of Jewish Christians who held to a basically Pharisee outlook. They maintained that, to be saved, you had first to be circumcised, and then trust in Jesus. They also advocated that Christians should keep every detail of the Old Testament law with regard to diet. Several sections in Paul's letters refer to these issues and the disagreement they caused in the Christian community.

This Pharisaical tendency has remained in the church down the centuries and has never totally disappeared from it. It is still with us to this day, and is arguably the dominant form of Christianity, even though it misses the whole point of Jesus' life and message.

There was, of course, one Pharisee who definitely made it all the way. He made a complete break with his Pharisee past and began to enjoy to the full the result of the new birth and freedom from the performance orientation which was central to the Pharisee way of life. I'm referring to the apostle Paul. He wrote to the Christians in Philippi:

> "If anyone else thinks they have reason to put confidence in the flesh, I have more: circumcised on the eighth day, of the tribe of Benjamin, a Hebrew of Hebrews; in regard to the law, a Pharisee; as for zeal, persecuting the church; as for righteousness based on the law, faultless. But whatever were gains to me I now consider loss for the sake of Christ. (Philippians 3 v 4–7)

The Pharisee mind-set is difficult to eradicate. We need to be constantly on our guard against it. But the apostle Paul stands as a testimony to the fact that it is possible for Pharisees to change and to come to know the freedom and joy of the righteousness that comes by simple faith in Jesus and the goodness that flows from gratitude for forgiveness rather than being a manipulative attempt to win acceptance.

Chapter fourteen

New Wine and New Wineskins

If we are going to be faithful to Jesus as his disciples today, we need to be ruthless in rooting out Pharisee tendencies, first in ourselves, and then in the Christian community around us. It is no use saying we trust in Jesus and follow him if in fact we act like Pharisees. This means that many Christians need a fundamental change in the way they see and do things.

Early in Jesus' ministry some puzzled people came to Him with a question. They had noticed a difference between what the Pharisees did and what he and his disciples did. This difference raised questions in their minds, to which they wanted answers. The question they asked Jesus was this:

> "How is it that John's disciples and the disciples of the Pharisees are fasting, but yours are not?"
>
> (Mark 2 v 18)

Jesus' answer was typically enigmatic:

> "How can the guests of the bridegroom fast while he is with them? They cannot, so long as they have him with them. But the

> time will come when the bridegroom will be taken from them, and on that day they will fast.
>
> "No-one sews a patch of unshrunk cloth on an old garment. Otherwise, the new piece will pull away from the old, making the tear worse. And no-one pours new wine into old wineskins. Otherwise, the wine will burst the skins and both the wine and the wineskins will be ruined. No, they pour new wine into new wineskins." (Mark 2 v 19–22).

It would be interesting to know more about the background to the question. Why were John's disciples and the Pharisees fasting? What kind of fast was it? At the time of Jesus the practice of fasting was well-established in Jewish religion. Fasting, in the sense of going without food, came about because loss of appetite is often a side effect of grief. Refusal to eat then became a deliberate expression of sorrow in other contexts as well as bereavement. It became a sign of sorrow over past sin, and so of repentance. It also became an expression of sorrow over things which were not as they should be, and hence a form of prayer. Gradually these more spontaneous forms of fasting became institutionalised, and the Jews then established special days for fasting.

The Old Testament law only called for one fast. This was in connection with the annual Day of Atonement. But by Jesus' time many other fast days had crept into the Jewish Calendar. Many Jews, the Pharisees included, fasted twice every week, on Mondays and Thursdays. It says that John's disciples and the Pharisees fasted often, so it seems probable that we are not talking about the Day of Atonement here, more likely the other fast days. It seems that the Pharisees observed these but Jesus and his disciples didn't.

It is important to establish that Jesus was not opposed to fasting. After all, He began his ministry with a forty-day fast, and in the Sermon on the Mount he gave instructions about fasting in which he assumed his disciples would sometimes fast. In spite of this though, fasting was obviously not a noticeable feature in the life of Jesus or his followers. This absence of fasting was obvious enough to raise a question in people's minds.

So, what was Jesus' answer to the question? And why did he suddenly start talking about weddings and bridegrooms?

Jesus' reply, simply, was that for him and for his disciples, it was not an appropriate time to fast. The gist of his reply was that fasting is appropriate to mourning and he and the disciples are rejoicing. You fast at funerals and you feast at weddings. When you've lost someone you are unable to eat for sorrow. But when you've found someone you have lost, or discovered a new friend, you want to throw a party and invite everyone to come and meet them. "My disciples are not fasting," said Jesus, in effect, "because they are celebrating a gain, not mourning a loss. This is party time. Fasting is not appropriate."

What was the party for? The answer is there in the message Jesus was preaching. The synoptic gospel writers sum up his message in the words "The kingdom of God has drawn near", or as we saw in a previous chapter, "the kingdom of God has arrived". Throughout the gospels Jesus uses wedding imagery in connection with the kingdom of God. The kingdom, he says, is "like a man who throws a banquet because his son has got married" (see Matthew 22 v 1–41). The kingdom of God is like girls at a wedding, waiting with their lamps for the bridegroom to arrive to start the procession as he takes the bride back to his house (Matthew 25 v 1–13). Jesus is the bridegroom. He has come to claim his bride (the community of his disciples). His coming inaugurates a banquet of good things: victims are going to see their unrepentant oppressors get their just desserts; at the same time repentant sinners are going to be pardoned; those who welcome the King are going to be blessed with the Gift, and gifts, of the Holy Spirit; miracles of healing are going to take place; peace is going to break out as Jesus' followers put into practice his teaching about forgiveness. So it was entirely consistent with Jesus' message that he and the disciples should not fast.

However, Jesus warned that there would be a time when the bridegroom would be taken away. At that time the joy that accompanied the inauguration of the kingdom would be changed to earnest prayer for its completion and the return of the King. "When that time comes," Jesus says, "the bridegroom's friends will fast." This is where we stand today, in the "now, but not yet" phase of the Kingdom. The Kingdom is coming. In some senses and to some degree it is here already. But it is not complete. We feast because it is coming and we fast because it has only come in part. But the feasting outweighs the fasting because the end result is a foregone conclusion.

In 1945 people in Britain celebrated wildly when Victory in Europe was proclaimed. The nation's cities were still full of bomb sites. The war was still going on in the Far East. People were tired, hungry and grieving over the loss of loved ones or worried about those who had not yet returned home. Rationing was still in operation. The peace that people celebrated was not yet a full reality but they celebrated nevertheless because the decisive battle had been won. In a similar way, we celebrate because Jesus has won the decisive battle. Even though we still suffer the consequences of Satan's rule over the human race, we are celebrating victory. Fasting and feasting sum up the basic divergence between the Pharisees' approach and Jesus' approach. Self-denial, self-discipline and self-control are at the root of the Pharisee mindset. Sorrow is the Pharisee's starting point. The world, as the Pharisee sees it, is in a terrible condition. Sin is rife and on the increase. The forces of evil are gathering, things are in an awful state and getting worse by the minute – and it is down to us to do something about it. We have to resist the downward slide by self-discipline and attention to law and order. That's the way Pharisees see things, and the way they respond to what they see – lay down the law to others, and make sure you keep it yourself. Hold back the tide of evil through discipline and self-control.

But Jesus starts from a different point. Things are bad, but not as bad as they seem. They never can be as long as God remains. This is still the world God created and that He pronounced as good. There is sin and sickness in the world, but God is acting to do something about it. The Kingdom has come and is coming more and more. There is a judgement to come and none of us will be able to stand guiltless before God, but there is also mercy and pardon for repentant sinners, and the power of the Spirit to help them change their ways. God is forming a new community of his children, those who know him, love him, have confessed their sin and turned from it, who are working with him to create a new society. There is hope.

The Pharisee panics about the growing tide of evil and desperately tries through human effort to hold it back. Jesus starts from a place of confidence and hope in God. Fasting comes naturally to Pharisees. It flows appropriately from their basically paranoid, pessimistic outlook. But the coming, through Jesus, of the Kingdom of God, is cause for feasting. That is not to say that there is no place at all for fasting in the thinking of Jesus and his followers – someone who is full of love cannot help but experience sadness at the state of mankind. Yet constantly the sin and unhappiness of the human race is brought into relationship with God's action through Jesus. This always, without exception, brings hope and a sense of joy and celebration which we can express more appropriately in a *fiesta* than in a fast.

For Jesus' disciples to be fasting in the way that the Pharisees and John's disciples were doing, would have meant imposing onto the new situation of the kingdom irrelevant patterns of behaviour which had been consistent with a situation which was now past. These patterns of behaviour have become unhelpful and inappropriate in the new situation of the Kingdom of God. They are like pouring new wine into old wineskins or putting a new patch on an old garment – both actions that were inappropriate and destructive. In the same way, we need to realise that the old wineskins and old patches of Pharisee religion are inappropriate to real Christianity.

This thought of applying inappropriate old structures to the new life of the kingdom crops up in several of Jesus parables and sayings. We have already noted in a previous chapter, that Jesus warned about the leaven of the Pharisees. Another example occurs in Matthew 22 v 11–12, at the end of Matthew's version of the parable of the wedding banquet:

> "But when the king came in to see the guests, he noticed a man there who was not wearing any wedding clothes. He asked, 'How did you get in here without wedding clothes, friend?' The man was speechless. Then the king told the attendants, 'Tie him hand and foot, and throw him outside, into the darkness, where there will be weeping and gnashing of teeth.' For many are invited, but few are chosen."

People have viewed the wedding garment in this parable in different ways. Here are two explanations that are often given:

1. The wedding garment represents repentance. On this understanding the problem is that the man is trying to pass himself off as a Christian without truly repenting.

2. The wedding garment represents the imputed righteousness of Jesus Christ. On this understanding the man's clothes represent the "filthy rags" of human righteousness. This man is trusting in his own goodness instead of trusting in Jesus' death as the means of his salvation.

According to the first view the point of the parable is that you can't be saved without repentance. The other view makes the point that you can't come to God except through Jesus. However, I believe there is more to it than either of these suggestions.

The important point here is that the clothes the man is wearing are inappropriate for the occasion. The parable is making the same point as the sayings about patches and wineskins. It is about the inappropriateness of old ways in the light of the new experience of the kingdom of God. The ordinary clothing represents an attitude which plays down or ignores the kingdom of God. Repentance and trust in Christ's atoning work are, of course, both part of the appropriate response to the kingdom. But a Pharisaical repentance which is just a matter of applying self-effort to keep the rules isn't. You can do the right things, and believe the right things, in terms of intellectual assent, but still not be wearing the wedding garment.

The wedding garment represents:

- Humbly acknowledging your own inadequacy;
- Lovingly acclaiming the king;
- Gratefully and joyfully submitting to his authority, and
- Depending on his mercy and power to help you.

The man without the wedding garment wasn't doing any of those things. He was simply relying on his own goodness to be acceptable to God. This was inappropriate and unacceptable in a situation where forgiveness was being offered through Jesus' death. The parable of the bridesmaids in Matthew 25 may be making a similar point. The bridesmaids who are relying on their own, inadequate supplies of goodness are excluded from the wedding banquet of the Kingdom of God.

So there are ways of behaving which fit comfortably with Pharisee religion but are inappropriate for God's kingdom. To represent these, Jesus uses the imagery of the old garment, the old wineskin, the yeast in the pure dough, the working clothes worn to a wedding, or the inadequate supply of oil in the bridesmaid's lamp.

What are these inappropriate ways of behaving? That is a dangerous question. As we ask it, we are in the position of the person playing "Snakes and Ladders" who before reaching "home" has to get past the last snake which could send them sliding right down to the bottom of the board. We could so easily list various aspects of the right behaviour and set it up as a new law to be obeyed in a Pharisaical way. To give a small example, joy is an obvious and appropriate response to what God has done for us in Jesus' but we can't turn this into a law, making people feel guilty if they come to church feeling depressed or grieving. If joy doesn't come from the heart, it is hypocritical to fake it.

With that caution, then, let's go on to look at the things which constitute the new wine, the new cloth, the wedding garment, and the fresh oil – the appropriate responses to the kingdom. We shall do this first on a personal level, looking at our individual responses, and then on a corporate level, looking at the structures and behaviour of the church.

In spite of what I have just said, **sadness** is obviously one inappropriate response to the Kingdom of God. That's not to say that Christians will never grieve or be unhappy. We will go through unpleasant and painful experiences like everyone else. But there will be a difference in the way we grieve. As Paul said we will not grieve, , "like the rest of the human race, who have no hope." (I Thessalonians 4 v 13). There will be sadness and regret, but always relieved by hope and confidence in God.

Guilt is another old garment that needs to be discarded, because you can't put a kingdom patch on it. Pharisee religion is full of false guilt and designed to make people guilty so that they will turn away from sin. Christian Churches are full of guilty people. They've heard God's law. They've read what Jesus said in the Sermon on the Mount and they have been subjected to endless guilt-producing sermons exhorting them to give more, witness more, be better parents and be more concerned for the poor. They know that they have blown it, and they feel guilty. They are repenting, in their own strength, as hard as they know how, but they keep failing. They fail to witness to their colleagues at work. They fail to resist the temptation to watch pornographic TV programmes. When cornered by an embarrassing accusation they lie to protect their skin. They fail to be faithful in marriage. And finally, they fail to forgive others who hurt them by their failures.

But there is no place for guilt in the Kingdom of God. The Church is not full of saints. It is full of people who are sinners but wanting not to be. Jesus did not come to get us condemned, but to get us rescued. God knows what we are made of. He knows we are dust. In mercy he sent Jesus to take the punishment so we can be forgiven. He offers the Holy Spirit to help us do better. Of course God doesn't want us to sin but, when we do, he doesn't want us to be guilty, either. He wants us to confess that we have sinned, ask His forgiveness, receive it, pick ourselves up and carry on, watching out next time the temptation comes, so that we can avoid it, with his help. If we fail again, however often, he wants us to keep trying. Since he forgives us, he expects us to forgive ourselves.

Trying to gain approval is another inappropriate response to the Kingdom of God. You can't pour the new wine of the kingdom into the old wineskin of performance orientation. God accepts you. He loves you. He gives you the privilege of being his child. Once you acknowledge his Kingship and hand control of your life over to him, you become his representative – his servant. There is no more prestigious position. You do not need to creep and crawl or try to impress others. In every situation you can act as what you are, showing mercy to others from your own position of acceptance and security in God's love.

Finally, in the 'individual' section, **condemnation of others** is an inappropriate way of behaving in a Kingdom context. God alone has the right to judge us and before him we all stand equally condemned. Without his mercy we have no hope. We stand condemned before him, not just for wrong things we have done deliberately and obviously, but for what we are in ourselves and for things we have thought and intended even in our apparently "good" actions. Rejection and condemnation are what we deserve from God. But what he offers us is mercy.

Once you realise all this, it means you can no longer pass judgement on anyone else or condemn them. This is not the right time, you are not the right person, and since you are yourself a sinner in need of God's mercy, you are in no place to condemn anyone else. On the other hand, receiving God's mercy sets you free to pass it on – or at least it should do, as Jesus pointed out in the parable of the unforgiving servant (see Matthew 18 v 23–35). This doesn't mean that we can never warn people when they seem to be breaking God's law. It doesn't mean that there will never be a place for Church discipline. However it does mean that, when we are involved in correcting others, it will always be with a sense of humility and an awareness of our own vulnerability – and it will be just that, correcting sinners, not rejecting them, not turning them away or looking down on them, not trying to do God's work by punishing them ourselves.

We have to work this out in the context of our corporate life as members of Christ's Body. We need to eradicate the leaven of the Pharisees from our churches. We can patch up the old Pharisee religion and try to join it to Christianity but it will not fit. We can pour the new wine of the gospel into the old structure of Pharisee religion, but the gospel always bursts through its restrictions.

The gospel demands a new way of being God's people. We need "unleavened" churches from which the yeast of the Pharisees is decisively excluded. Even in our religiously ignorant society there are plenty of people outside the Christian church who have read enough of the New Testament to know something about Jesus and about the Pharisees. They know enough to respond positively to Jesus. They like him. They also know enough not to think much of the Pharisees – and what they see too often in the church is the "leaven of the Pharisees" at work. So, both from the point of view of pleasing God, and of reaching non-Christians with the gospel, it is vital that we do all we can to remove the "leaven of the Pharisees" from our midst. But what happens when we do? What difference will it make?

As we have seen, the main features of Pharisee religion are:

- outward compliance to laws without attention to inward morality;
- a motive of seeking acceptance and approval from God and others;
- a resulting tendency to hypocrisy – people concealing their true motives and feelings to avoid condemnation.

In contrast, Jesus modelled and advocated a new approach which put the emphasis on internal goodness and on allowing the Gospel and the Holy Spirit to change our thoughts and motives. He encouraged honesty and openness. He offers a new motive of gratitude for the mercy that God has already given us through the cross.

Imagine a church where people can trust that they will not be condemned, criticised or disfellowshipped if they own up to sinful thoughts and feelings, or even to sinful acts.

Imagine a church where, within proper safeguards, people are openly encouraged to share the worst about themselves – where James' instruction: "Confess your sins to one another, and pray for one another so that you may be healed" is taken literally.

Imagine a church where people know they will not be gossiped about or criticised behind their back, or publicly humiliated. A church where, without condoning sin, people freely admit to sins and failings, even of the most dreadful kind. Imagine, furthermore, that this honest and compassionate church is one where people have true goals for goodness and where the members are bound together by a solemn covenant to pursue an ambitious inward righteousness and help one another to attain it. Picture a church where, instead of trying to please the Pastor, or that awkward pressure group who will make things difficult if they don't get their own way, everyone is wanting to please God. That's an unleavened church.

There are a number of important distinguishing features which make up an unleavened church:

Absence of judgement and condemnation

The main reason why we don't find this kind of openness in most churches today is simply that people are afraid of being condemned, criticised, gossiped about, and rejected. The reason why they are afraid is because they know this is the way most church communities treat people. Each person thinks, "I've seen other people raise their heads above the wall and get fired at, so I'm not going to risk the same fate myself."

Tens of thousands of Christians, inside the hidden recesses of their mind, are saying to themselves something like this:

"I saw what happened to that innocent new Christian who shared their problem openly in the housegroup. And I am going to make sure it doesn't happen to me. To be sure, I joined in the 'tut-tutting', and the gossip myself, and I kept quiet during the angry 'that shouldn't be allowed' discussions, but that only means I can't expect to be treated any differently if I fail. So I'm going to try hard to keep my record clean – and when I blow it, I'm going to hide and pretend and deceive others into thinking that I am a perfect Christian."

That's unfortunately the story in many churches. Professing Christians beat their wives (or husbands!) abuse their children, lose their tempers, masturbate, smoke or drink more than they should in secret. People break their wedding vows, engage in dishonest business deals at work, and then come to church, feeling guilty and insecure, wishing they could find the strength and courage to be different. Afraid of rejection and condemnation (yet longing for acceptance and understanding) they put on an act of being good Christians. Each person in the congregation thinks they are the only one with problems. The only person who may have some inkling of the reality is the Pastor, who hears some of their confessions. But Pastors themselves are often prisoners of the system, trapped by the fear that if they were totally open about their own failings, they might lose their their livelihood – in some cases their home as well.

What is needed is people, especially leaders, who will take the risk of being open. But first of all we need to declare war on those attitudes which mitigate against openness: judgement, condemnation, ridicule, and gossip.

"But surely," some people will say, "if you don't condemn people when they sin, you are condoning what they do!" Of course that isn't the case. There is no contradiction whatever between maintaining a high ideal of morality yourself, yet refusing to condemn those who fail to keep it. You can teach a high standard without rejecting those who don't measure up to it. We can associate together on the basis that our aim is to help each other to be more and more like Jesus, and still be patient and compassionate with one another when we fail.

We can encourage each other to righteousness and even exercise church discipline without rejecting and humiliating one another. Jesus himself showed us how in Matthew 18 v15ff, where He presents a non-Pharisee way of dealing with another person's failings and sins. "Go and point out their fault, just between the two of you," says Jesus. Not to humiliate him, to condemn or reject him, but to "win your brother or sister back". We have already looked at this passage in chapter eight.

Jesus' instructions in this passage end with, "If they refuse to listen to the church, treat them as you would a pagan or a tax collector."

The normal practise of Jesus' hearers at the time would have been to ostracise pagans and tax collectors and have nothing to do with them. That might be what Jesus intends us to understand in this saying. However, in the "Great Commission" Jesus commands us to "make disciples of all nations". Christians don't ostracise pagans or even tax-collectors. They try to convince them of the truth of the gospel and to bring them to acknowledge Jesus as Lord. We should first make it plain to them that they are no longer part of the Christian community but, rather than rejecting them totally, we should treat that person as if they were an unbeliever and start sharing the first principles of God's grace and of the gospel with them all over again.

Sometimes it is right for Christian disciples to withdraw fellowship from someone who is sinning and to disassociate themselves publicly from that person's actions – but only when they have tried everything else and the person concerned still refuses to listen.

I believe the absence of loving church discipline based on Matthew 18: 15–22 is one of the main reasons for the prevalence of both immorality and Pharisaism in the church. We allow each other's sins to go unchecked, but show our dismay and disapproval by gossip, or sarcastic remarks, or by rejecting and humiliating those who have failed. In the process we empower a destructive cycle of condemnation, concealment, deceit, more sin, and further condemnation.

There are two unfortunate spin-offs of Pharisaism in the church. One is that sinners outside the church assume they will not be welcome inside, because of the kind of life they lead. The other is that those people outside the church who like to think of themselves as upright and moral see the gap between the Church's moral pronouncements and Christians' immoral behaviour and draw the conclusion that all Christians are hypocrites. Jesus' way of doing things will lead us to a place where:

- Sinners know and feel that they will be welcomed, loved and helped in the church, and, at the same time,
- the church regains its credibility, because the gap between what it says and what it does has been removed.

So an unleavened church will be one where sin is condemned, but people aren't; where sinners are welcome, provided they want to become saints, and the only reason for being excluded is that you have refused to listen to your fellow Christians. It will be a church where people are merciful towards each other's failings and sins, and honest about their own and where people deal with problems face to face rather than sweeping them under the carpet or making them the subject of gossip.

In addition, an unleavened church will also be a church where people are set free from petty restrictions and peer pressure to toe the line of man-made norms, because everyone's gaze is fixed on what God wants, not what they want.

Chapter fifteen

The Swing of the Pendulum

In this final chapter we turn to look at the influence of Pharisaism in the church today.

As we have already noticed, another influential group of people often hovered in the background while Jesus and the Pharisees clashed. The Sadducees were the Pharisees' great rivals. The two groups represented opposite poles of mainline Judaism in Jesus' day. The rivalry between the two groups has many similarities with the division in modern Protestant Christianity between 'Evangelicals' and 'Liberals'. Both involve opposition between what we might today describe as left wing and right wing outlooks.

You could easily compare the Pharisees to the right wing conservatives of the present day, with regard to both theology and politics.They wanted to keep things as they had been in the past. They were fiercely nationalistic, and concerned about issues of law and order. I have the feeling that, if they were around today, they would be giving their support to campaigns to strengthen the police-force and bring back the death penalty. They would oppose pornography, abortion and (being Jewish!) Saturday trading. Theologically they believed in the authority of the Bible, in angels and demons and the resurrection of the dead. In the

USA today a typical Pharisee might well be Republican and Southern Baptist. His British counterpart might be Tory and Plymouth Brethren.

On the other hand, the Sadducees were more liberal. Like the Pharisees they believed firmly in keeping the law of Moses, but they rejected the body of additional laws and interpretations of the law which the Pharisees held to. The Sadducees enjoyed sampling other cultures, they were more willing to live and let live, and they didn't believe in the supernatural, or the resurrection of the dead.
If we take the two groups as symbolising the left and the right, politically and theologically (the comparison doesn't quite fit, but is useful), it is interesting to note that both groups worshipped God, and presumably, since they both thought they were right, they each claimed God for their side. However, Jesus refused to give his allegiance to either. Neither group was able to claim the authority of the Son of God for their cause. That suggests to me that neither of the equivalent present-day extremes of liberal and fundamentalist, or capitalist and socialist, can claim divine authority for their beliefs and traditions.

Over the last few decades I have noticed a swing of the pendulum in Western society away from "left wing" Sadducee attitudes and back towards a "right-wing", Pharisee mentality. This has happened on both sides of the Atlantic, both in society as a whole and in the Christian world, and it makes it essential for Christians to pay attention to the warnings that Jesus gave about the "leaven of the Pharisees". Too often Christians are guilty of following trends in society instead of shaping them – listening to their neighbours more than listening to God. If we are truly to have a prophetic edge we need to be going against the flow.

This is true whatever the dominant outlook in our culture may be. When right wing nationalism is in fashion we will tell people how racial barriers are broken down in the body of Christ, and how the law of the kingdom of God demands that we share what God has given us with one another and care for the poor. When socialism is in vogue, we shall be campaigning for each individual's personal responsibility to God, and for the divine creativity expressed in different cultures. To Liberals we emphasise the authority of Scripture. To Evangelicals we stress social concern and the power of the Holy Spirit; among Charismatics we emphasise the importance of using the brain God gave us, and so on.

This current swing of the pendulum is part of an ongoing process which can be traced back through several centuries, as far back as the "Enlightenment" period of the 18th century. During the intervening time there has been a succession of cultural movements, each of which has involved a contrary reaction to the one before. The Enlightenment was in many ways a "Sadducee" period. People prided themselves on being intellectually sophisticated. The deist view of God which was popular at the time saw God as a clockmaker who had created the universe and set it in motion but had no ongoing involvement with it. The supernatural was out of fashion and people tried to be ruled by reason.

Romanticism started as a reaction to the intellectualism of the Enlightenment. In art and literature this movement was characterised by a more emotional response to the world and a fascination with the supernatural. It had its religious counterpart first in Germany in Pietism and the Moravian Movement, then in America in the religious revivals led by Jonathan Edwards and in Britain by George Whitefield and John Wesley, along with the Evangelical movement in the Church of England. Within the course of a hundred years not only Britain but the whole world was transformed. Enthusiastic, Bible believing Christianity became popular throughout the English-speaking world and was spread elsewhere by the rapidly growing missionary movement. Between them, low church Evangelicalism and high church Anglo-Catholicism brought spiritual life to the Church of England while the "Non-Conformist conscience became a force to be reckoned with in British politics and preachers like Charles Spurgeon had the ear of the nation. A vibrant Evangelical Christianity with the grace of God at its heart became the dominant faith of the Victorian era, both in Britain and in the USA. However, there was also another story, well illustrated by the novels of Charles Dickens. As the century wore on, the molten lava of Evangelical Christianity, which continued to flow powerfully through British and American society, began to cool and harden at the edges into a hypocritical and condemning legalism with a Pharisaical outlook.

As the nineteenth century movement of spiritual renewal and life reached its peak, a counter movement emerged, coming from two directions. In Germany a new approach to the study of the Bible, called Higher Criticism, began to question the divine inspiration of the Bible, and in Britain, atheist academics eagerly seized on Darwin's theory of natural selection and used it as an argument against divine creation. Intellectual scepticism came back into fashion and science began to be given the awe and reverence that had previously been reserved for religion. Sadducee intellectualism was in vogue once more. At the same time, as the Christian church grew strong, it also grew fat. People failed to distinguish between Christianity and Christendom. The famous missionary, David Livingstone, declared that he went to Africa to open up the continent "for commerce and Christianity". Many people's Christianity was becoming an inherited tradition rather than a personal conviction. The tide of faith ebbed, leaving people with a rigid moral code which was no longer based on belief.

From the early twentieth century onwards church attendance declined rapidly in Britain and in most other European nations, while the main denominations became, for the most part, liberal in their theology. In society as a whole this was the period in which socialism and communism made their greatest progress. Judaeo-Christian morality, based on the Ten Commandments, remained the accepted norm, even in the Communist countries of the East, where the State simply took God's place as the object of people's loyalty and the definer of right and wrong. In Britain, "Victorian" morality continued but was now deprived of the spiritual passion which had motivated it during the revivals in the previous century. It became no more than a cold legalism. As real Christianity declined, Pharisaism replaced it. By the 1920s and 30s, in most churches, the legalist "social gospel", based on the idea of the Fatherhood of God and the brotherhood of man, had replaced the gospel of grace that had warmed Wesley's heart and set the world on fire. The leaven of the Pharisees was all that was left.

Moral standards are often eroded in war time, and the second world war was no exception. Husbands and wives were separated from one another and placed in close proximity to other people in life or death situations. With the risk of death threatening every day, a 'live for today' mentality took hold, and people no longer held so closely to the moral code which was still the accepted norm in society. This decline in moral standards continued throughout the '50s. By the end of the '50s young people were starting to notice a gap between the older generation's behaviour and the morals to which they gave verbal assent. Many older people began to change their morality to justify their own behaviour, while the rising generation questioned and rebelled against the hypocrisy of their parents. This change of outlook partly involved a genuine revolt against pharisaical legalism. People were no longer content to be told what was right and wrong without being given reasons for it. Situational ethics became the fashion, encouraging people to look at results rather than rules as their guide to good behaviour and the 'sixties and 'seventies became a more sceptical 'Sadducee' period. The Church, surprised by the results of its own failure, no longer had a unique message to share. Church attendance went into a steep decline.

However, even in this atmosphere, Pharisaism raised its head in a new form. As the old morality was abandoned, a new morality emerged to take its place. Hypocrisy came to be regarded as the most serious sin, closely followed by racial prejudice. Honesty, sincerity and tolerance became the most prized virtues, replacing those of a former generation which had majored on loyalty, respect for authority and thrift. An amazing change came about in public attitudes to homosexual sex. In the1950s homosexuality was regarded as a personal choice and was illegal. By 2012 Homosexuality was popularly regarded as genetically conditioned, homosexual sex was regarded as normal and the British Association for Counselling and Therapy had ruled that it was unethical for its members to offer therapy to help someone change their gender orientation. Although the public attitude to the issue had radically changed, the same condemning Pharisaism lay behind both attitudes.

Before long, the results of this massive erosion of traditional moral standards began to be seen and there started to be a backlash with many people saying, in effect, "This has gone far enough!"

In Britain, Margaret Thatcher's rule as Prime Minister was the start of the turn round. She began once again to stress "old fashioned" values such as thrift, hard work and patriotic fervour. About the same time the Reagan years in the United States began to see the rise of the "moral majority" movement. The appearance of the AIDS virus brought a change to the easy-going sexual morality of the nineteen sixties and seventies. As the eighties came to an end, we began to see the emergence into responsible adulthood of the first children who had grown up in a permissive society, many of them carrying the emotional scars of their parents' divorces, not to mention their own survival through the turmoil of sexual promiscuity, abortion or drug and alcohol abuse.

The permissive ethics that had become the norm during the '60s and '70s, combined with the economic deprivation experienced by the poorest members of society in the '80s and '90s, produced social conditions which resulted in a rise in petty crime and outbreaks of civil unrest. These in turn set those who were more comfortably off calling for a clampdown.

The turn around from a Sadducee outlook to Pharisaism really began to take root with the Conservative party's "Back to Basics" campaign in 1992. The media turned it into a fiasco for the government but it touched a nerve in society among people who had had enough of permissiveness and wanted to see a return to discipline and order. The media had a field day exposing sexual misdemeanours and hypocrisy in high places but even these exposures were an expression of a public demand for something more than a slogan.

Back to Basics marked a quite sudden turn of the tide in British society that took many by surprise. Government ministers who were still heading down the road that the permissive society had signposted met Prime Minister John Major and a hoard of newspaper editors coming the other way. They were confused to be condemned for being immoral rather than praised for embracing freedom.

Christians throughout the world find ourselves today in a basically Pharisaical society. It is a confusing time. Morally weary from swimming against the tide through the years of Sadducee liberalism, many Christians are not sure which way we should be heading now that Pharisee legalism is back in vogue. The confusion is complicated by the fact that an essentially Judaeo-Christian "law" is rapidly being replaced in Western society by a Secular Humanist law which is similar in some areas but different in others. Christians feel a need to take a stand but aren't sure whether to respond as Sadducees or Pharisees, whether to dig in their heels or to live and let live.

In this moral climate it is easy for Christians to jump on the Pharisee bandwagon and add their voice to the condemnation around them. But we need to be wise and look before we leap. All too often the church has been guilty of following the trends in society instead of shaping them and situations where Christians follow social trends tend to be dangerous and deceptive. In the present social climate we can all too easily find ourselves, like the Pharisees in Jesus' day, supporting "traditions of men". The current swing towards traditional values is selective. It is towards the punishment of criminals but not towards mercy for those who repent. It is towards integrity and honesty but not towards care for the poor and keeping the Sabbath. It is towards faithfulness in marriage but tolerates cohabitation beforehand and homosexual marriage for those who prefer.

Often it's not in relation to the "big" issues that we feel the tension most strongly. Christians can join in lobbies and put pressure on governments if they choose to, or just keep quiet and not join in if there are issues on which we aren't so sure. It is when moral decisions come close to home that we face the greatest heart searching.

Take the question of Sunday trading, for instance. Do you refuse to work on a Sunday, or agree to do so for the sake of keeping your job? Do you lobby and make protests, or just avoid working or shopping on a Sunday and let the rest of the world make its own choice? Or do you abandon the Christian Sunday altogether and treat it just like any other day apart from going to a church service?

The issues are particularly acute when families are divided between Christian and secular morality (or even between different moral stances between Christians). How does a Christian mother and grandmother who wants to live according to the Bible respond to a daughter who is in a lesbian relationship? How do Christian parents respond to an adult son who wants to bring his girlfriend or partner home for a weekend and expects to share a bed with her? What do you say to a woman who has become a Christian, having lived with the same man for ten years and born his children? Do you say, "You must leave him and move out," or "You are effectively married, make it legal by having a wedding?" Where is the line that separates negative, condemning Pharisaism from maintaining integrity and standing up for Biblical truth? In general terms, when others break God's laws, should Christians preach and protest or simply live according to God's principles themselves, leaving others to follow their own conscience (or lack of it)?

An important starting point for Christians is to realise that the issue in present-day society is not one of lawlessness over against God's law. There are very few truly lawless people. Even thieves have their codes of conduct. Our society is not without values and morals.They differ from those of past generations but they exist, nevertheless, and are very powerful.

Previous generations valued respect for authority, along with trustworthiness, hard work and loyalty. People may not value those things in quite the same way today, but they do value sincerity, tolerance and respect for other people's liberty. A previous generation condemned divorce and adultery. Today's generation condemns racism, sexism, and ageism. Some of these values, both new and old, are Biblical. Others, like patriotism and homosexual marriage, are more debatable. Christians need to learn to give credit where credit is due, rather than being too quick to condemn. We also need to realise that, whatever moral standpoints people hold in today's society, they hold them, not because they are God's law or the teaching of Jesus Christ, but because those morals are either traditional or fashionable. We need to realise that, whether the moral 'laws' that people around us hold coincide with God's laws or not, they are in fact being held as traditions of men. A good law kept in reverence to social pressure or cultural tradition is an idol, however good it is. This is the kind of righteousness that God described through Isaiah as "filthy rags". Christians are not called to support the traditions of men but to advance the kingdom rule of God. Our main aim is not to make people toe the line but to open their eyes to the Lordship of Jesus.

In the present day climate, those who love Jesus and want to follow him will want to expose the secular Pharisaism of our society for what it is. We will want to help people acknowledge the ill-considered value-judgements they make without realising what they are really saying. We will want to bring people to acknowledge the existence of the false "gods" which have forced those values on them. More than anything else we will want to make sure that we ourselves are not duped into losing God's most precious gift to us, the gift of grace which cost the life-blood of his only Son. We have to constantly make sure that our religion represents the grace of our Lord Jesus Christ and not the leaven of the Pharisees. This means that, in every situation, we need to start with the question "How would Jesus handle this?" I would suggest five principles that we can apply to avoid Pharisaism – principles which seem to me to be consistent with all we have learned in this book from Jesus' confrontations with the Pharisees.

1. Be true to God, and to yourself as his servant.

The Pharisees were over-sensitive to the opinions of men. In contrast, Jesus never let Himself be pushed around by peer pressure, no matter where it came from. He refused to fit anyone's mould, except his Father's. We should be the same.

2. Shun manipulation and control

Jesus never allowed others to push him around, but equally, he never manipulated or bullied other people. He never exerted pressure of any kind on other people to make them do what was right. The Pharisees used social pressure and manipulation to persuade people to toe the line but Jesus always left people free to choose, even when they made the wrong choices. We too have to avoid manipulation and pressure, leaving people free to choose, even when making the wrong choices leads them into sinful and destructive situations.

3. Be willing to warn others

Although we need to respect people's freedom, we do have a responsibility to point out to people the error of their ways and to lovingly warn them against wrong decisions and the consequences of those decisions. If there is a danger that I am aware of, I have a responsibility to warn people of it. If I am standing near the edge of a cliff and someone walks by me towards the edge without me warning them, I am partly responsible if they suffer injury or death as a result. The line between asserting pressure and stating an opinion is sometimes a difficult one to walk but we must not duck our responsibility towards other people.

4. Be willing to pay the price.

There will be a cost in living according to Jesus' laws in this world. It may be a cost of self-denial, or it may be the cost of rejection, ridicule and even persecution. Whatever the cost may be, as Christians, we cannot shrink from it. Jesus calls us to "take up our cross daily."

5. Constantly check our motives

Whatever choices we make, we need to constantly check our motives. It is so easy to behave in what we assume to be the right way because we always have done or because that's what society tells us. It is easy to follow the social norm because we want acceptance and affirmation from other people – but the only goodness that counts is that which springs from a heart of love. The only right motive for goodness is that we love God.

As Christians, our purpose and aim in life is to give glory to God. But we need to understand that our goodness does not give him glory. God is not glorified when we try hard to live according to his commands – we are. God is glorified by the fact that he forgives us and has mercy on us even though we do not deserve it. God is glorified by everything we do to show our gratitude for his grace and mercy. He is glorified when his power is shown through us and people see him changing us through His Spirit.

Trying hard makes us Pharisees. Trusting, believing, and responding to God in Jesus makes us his children, a sign of hope to a lost world and a testimony to his power and goodness. True repentance is not a change from being bad in our own strength to being good in our own strength. That was the big mistake the Pharisees made. True repentance involves a change from self-sufficiency to dependence on God. That change is the starting point of the Christian life. Dependence on God is the essence of Christianity from start to finish. The Pharisees had difficulty understanding this and they ended up missing God's plan for them, working against God and even crucifying his Son. Even though we may have the best of motives, the same can happen to us unless we are careful to "beware of the leaven of the Pharisees", as Jesus warned us to.

Study Guide

The study guide in the following pages will enable you to use the book flexibly in the context of a homegroup or lent course. Some groups will want to take a chapter a week. Other groups might prefer to cover two chapters a week.

Introductory week

Distribute the books, explain how your group will be using it for the studies. Brief people to read Chapter 1 during the coming week and. thereafter, to read the relevant chapter (or chapters) during the week before the meeting.

Read the quotation from William Smith on page 9 to whet people's appetite and help them see how important it is to understand the issues at stake between Jesus and the Pharisees.

Pray for God to use the book and the course to do his work in you.

Chapter 2 The Heart of the Matter

Scripture

People rarely read the Sermon on the mount in one piece. Start the study this week by reading Matthew chapters 5, 6 and 7 in one go (you could divide it up among the people in your group so several people each read a section or, if you have someone with drama training, you could ask them to read all three chapters to the group.

Questions for discussion

What impact did it have on you to hear the Sermon on the Mount read in one go?

How do you feel about being lights to the world and the salt of the earth?

Which do you consider as more important:

1) What people do or why they do it?
2) Whether actions are legally right or whether they achieve a positive result?
3) Avoiding evil or promoting goodness?

Respond in prayer to what you have heard (continue to do this at the end of each week's discussion).

Chapter 3 – Why Be Good?

Scripture

Read Matthew 23 v 5–7

Questions for discussion

What motives can people have for keeping God's law?

Which motives are appropriate and which are inappropriate – and why?

What motivates the way you behave?

Chapter 4 – Praise and Blame

Scripture

Read *either* Luke 7 v 36–49 *or* John 7 v 53–8 v 11

Questions for discussion

Enjoyment of praise or fear of blame – which motivates your behaviour most?

Do the people around you most often use the language of praise or the language of blame? How does their attitude affect you? How can you change your own language?

What practical implications does Jesus' teaching about judging have for you?

Chapter 5 – Guilt By Association

Scripture

Read Luke 15

Questions

Are there people you try to avoid? If so, why? Do you think God would want you to be avoiding them?

This chapter in the book mentions three reasons why people go astray from God. What are they? (See page 46, page 47 and page 48).
Which of the three do you most readily identify with and why?

Chapter 6 – Good God!

Scripture

Read Luke 5 v 17–26

Questions

How do you view God?

How does this affect the way you approach him?

How does it affect your attitude to other people?

Are there any ways in which you might need to change your understanding of God's character?

Chapter 7 Letter and Spirit

Scripture

Read I Samuel 21 v 1–6 and Mark 2 v 23–27.

Questions for discussion

What commandments did David break in I Samuel 21 v 1–6?

Was there anything in his situation that made this acceptable?

How do you feel about the idea that there could be situations where it might be appropriate to break one of God's laws in order to achieve a higher good?

Can you think of any ethical situations where that could be the case?

Chapter 8 – Test Cases

Scripture

Read and compare Matthew 12 v 9–14, Mark 3 v 1–6 and Luke 6 v 6–11.

Questions for Discussion

Why did the Pharisees become so angry about Jesus healing the man on the Sabbath?

Why were they wrong?

What is the purpose of God's Law?

Chapter 9 – The Conflict

Scripture

Read Matthew 12 v 22–37 and Matthew 22 v 15–33

Questions for discussion

What strikes you, as you read these passages?

Have any group members ever had a situation where they were put on the spot with a difficult question? How did they respond?

How did Jesus demonstrate his wisdom in responding to the Pharisees and the Sadducees?

Where were the Pharisees going wrong?

Where were the Sadducees going wrong?

Is there a risk of you going wrong in similar ways? How can you avoid this?

Chapter 10 – The seven Woes

Scripture

Read Matthew 23, Philippians 3 v 4–7

Questions for discussion

The seven woes address seven aspects of the Pharisees' behaviour. Quickly summarise these.

How much do you think these behaviours are present in the church today? Can you think of particular examples? In each case how do we avoid these behaviours?

How can we help to correct these behaviours when we see them in other people?

"Take from the altar of the past the fire and not the ashes." – what would that imply for you and for your church?

Chapter 11 – The Showdown

Scripture

Read John 11 v 45–57

Questions for discussion

What was the fear that motivated the Pharisees and the chief priests?

What does this show about their motives and priorities?

Have you ever wanted someone "out of the way" because they stop you achieving what you want? How should you respond in that kind of situation?

Chapter 12 – Beware the Leaven of the Pharisees

Scripture

Read Luke 12 v 1–5

Questions for discussion

What does the "leaven of the Pharisees" consist of?

Why is it important to avoid it?

What issues and situations can make us vulnerable to the the leaven of the Pharisees?

How can we resist it?

Chapter 13 – Born Again

Scripture

Read John 3 v 1–17 and Philippians 3 v 4–29

Questions for discussion

What does it mean to be "born again"? How does the new birth come about and how does it show itself?

What difference did the new birth make to Paul?

Chapter 14 – New Wine and New Wineskins

Scripture

Read Mark 2 v 18–22 and Matthew 22 v 1–11

Questions for discussion

What inappropriate behaviours do the old cloth and the old wineskins represent? How will these cause damage to our Christian life and to the church?

What new behaviours do the wedding garments represent?

Are you wearing "wedding garments"?

Chapter 15 – The Swing of the Pendulum

Scripture

Read Romans 8 v 1–17

Questions for discussion

What "Sadducee" attitudes do you think are prevalent in society today?

What "Pharisee" attitudes do you think are prevalent in society today?

Do you agree that on balance we are living in a Pharisee society?

What ethical dilemmas do you face as you try to live as a Christian in todays world? In each case, what would be a Pharisee response to those dilemmas and what response would Jesus want you to have?

What Pharisee characteristics can you see at work in the community where you live? In your church fellowship?

How can we avoid being Pharisees today?

Pray for your church or Christian Community, asking God to help you recognise Pharisee attitudes and to work to remove them.

By the same author:

Christian

First Things First

A fresh look at the first 11 chapters of the Bible, from Creation to Abram's departure for Haran. *First Things First* rejects the fruitless arguments that have gone on between scientific and religious fundamentalists and approaches these stories as inspired literature full of fabulous treasures of wisdom and insight. These early chapters of the Bible challenge our own culture and pose the question, "Where did human creativity come from?" The author proposes that the "days" of Genesis 1 are not literal 24 hour periods and argues that we are currently still in day six with day seven still to come.

The Heart of Christmas

A series of 13 cameo word sketches and meditations that bring the heart of Christmas to light through the eyes, ears and hearts of those it happened to. A great Christmas gift or an aid to help you prepare yourself to welcome the New Born King into your heart and home at Christmas.

Secular

Encounters on a Bus

You never know who you'll meet on a bus. In this collection of short stories the lives of the characters funnel through the same half hour bus journey and build, jigsaw-fashion, into a kind of novel – but one that goes sideways through space rather than forward through time. It's about different perspectives, about the way we meet but don't meet and how apparently chance encounters can change your life.

All these books can be purchased online from www.lulu.com

www.ingramcontent.com/pod-product-compliance
Ingram Content Group UK Ltd.
Pitfield, Milton Keynes, MK11 3LW, UK
UKHW020129250726
13967UKWH00002B/559

9 780956 581846